With one eye on the
too close for comfo
ducked under the rope which said
NO STUDENTS BEYC POINT. As soon as they reached the corner they heard it – the sound, as Danny said afterwards, of fearsome fishwifing. Vanessa's voice, pitched low and obviously intended as a whisper, nevertheless reached them quite clearly: 'Of all the *gut*less, *spine*less, *use*less –'

Danny and Kate exchanged glances.

'Novel way to go over lines,' said Danny.

Ned and Vanessa fight about virtually everything, so Kate knows it's a signal for open warfare when they are picked to act opposite each other. Once Vanessa gets an idea into her head there's no stopping her – and cool, secretive Ned is her latest victim. Somehow Vanessa is going to knock some sense into Ned – whatever the cost.

This is the first book in Jean Ure's lively and compelling trilogy about Kate, Danny, Vanessa and Ned, Arts and Drama students at a sixth form college.

Jean Ure is the acclaimed author of many books for young people, including YOU WIN SOME, YOU LOSE SOME and THE OTHER SIDE OF THE FENCE (nominated for the Carnegie Award), both available in the Freeway series.

Also by Jean Ure

THE OTHER SIDE OF THE FENCE
YOU WIN SOME, YOU LOSE SOME

Published by Corgi Freeway Books

Trouble With Vanessa

JEAN URE

CORGI
F·R·E·E·W·A·Y

TROUBLE WITH VANESSA
A CORGI FREEWAY BOOK 0 552 52428X

Originally published in Great Britain by Corgi Freeway Books

PRINTING HISTORY
Corgi Freeway edition published 1988

This book is set in 11/12 pt Palatino
by Colset Private Limited, Singapore.

Corgi Freeway Books are published by Transworld Publishers Ltd., 61–63 Uxbridge Road, Ealing, London W5 5SA, in Australia by Transworld Publishers (Australia) Pty. Ltd., 15–23 Helles Avenue, Moorebank, NSW 2170, and in New Zealand by Transworld Publishers (N.Z.) Ltd., Cnr. Moselle and Waipareira Avenues, Henderson, Auckland.

The publishers gratefully acknowledge permission to quote the following copyright material:
Extracts from *Voice and Speech in the Theatre* by Clifford Turner, Pitman Publishing.
'THE CARNIVAL IS OVER', © 1965 Chappell Music Limited. Words reproduced by permission.
Lines from 'The Waste Land' by T.S. Eliot, from *Collected Poems – 1909–1962*, Faber and Faber Limited.
'SINNER MAN', © Chappell Music Limited, Trad. Arr The Seekers words reproduced by permission.
Extract from 'Anthem from Doomed Youth' from THE COLLECTED POEMS OF WILFRED OWEN edited by C.D. Lewis. Reprinted by kind permission of Chatto & Windus, the estate of the author and the estate of the editor.

Made and printed in Great Britain by
Cox & Wyman Ltd., Reading, Berks.

TROUBLE WITH VANESSA

1

'Well, I think that just about wraps everything up.' Mr Slaney took his spectacles off, pinched the bridge of his nose between finger and thumb, put the spectacles back on again. He gazed at the new September intake: they gazed back at him, solemnly.

'Most of you,' said Mr Slaney, 'will have come to us direct from school. You'll find college life a little bit different . . . not quite as much supervision, perhaps, as you've been accustomed to. Not quite so many rules and regulations.'

Vanessa, standing in the front row, nudged at Kate with her elbow. Kate responded with an answering nudge.

'However,' went on Mr Slaney, 'extra freedom does bring extra responsibilities. You're all over sixteen, and we expect you to behave accordingly. That means working hard and playing sensibly.' He paused. 'I'm sure you all know everything there is to know about AIDS.'

AIDS? Kate blinked.

'If you don't, there are plenty of leaflets in the outer office. Don't be afraid to help yourselves to them. I know that for some of you, those that have come from single-sex establishments, this is going to be a new and – how shall we put it? – liberating experience. All I would say is, try not to let it go to your heads. In other words, behave responsibly. Use a bit of discretion, don't screw around.'

Kate bent her head, staring hard at the floor and her feet in their new red trainers. This was something else! Dear old Woodie (otherwise known as Miss Margaret Woodford, MA, Head of Parkhill High) would have died sooner than use language like that. *Screw around?* She probably didn't even know what the expression meant! As for AIDS, the mere thought of Woodie's prim, virginal lips even forming the word, never mind voicing it, was enough to bring one out in a rash.

Kate heard Woodie's thin, precise tones as she had heard them for the past five years at morning assembly: *Whatsoever things are pure, lovely, and of good report . . .*

The voice of Woodie mingled with that of Mr Slaney, telling them that if they *did* start a relationship, then 'just use a bit of common sense'.

Kate kept her head bent. Her cheeks by now were as red as her trainers. This, she thought, was Life with a Vengeance. This was what she had come here for. (She bet Vanessa wasn't blushing: Vanessa never did.)

'So there you are, that's it. I've said all I'm going to say. You'll find there's a copy of the master timetable on the notice board in the refectory, and another in the student's lounge. I suggest you spend the time between now and ten o'clock making a note of your classes and familiarizing yourselves with the layout of the place. If you have any problems, take them to your personal tutors; that's what they're there for. And just remember, whether you're going to be with us for one year or two, time passes a lot quicker than you think, so make the most of it!'

The room emptied as students piled out. Kate and Vanessa, being the furthest in, were amongst the last to leave.

'Where to?' said Vanessa. 'Lounge or refectory?'

A notice pointing up some stairs said REFECTORY; another, pointing along the corridor, said STUDENTS' LOUNGE. Before Kate could make her mind up, Vanessa had said 'Lounge' and set off along the corridor. Vanessa usually did make up her mind more quickly than Kate.

'Did you hear what he said about supervision? I told you it would be more mature than school! Nobody standing over you all the time.'

'And *boys*,' said Kate.

Boys everywhere. Boys all over the place. There were a couple now, walking just ahead of them. A black boy and a white boy. The white boy was tall, rangy, dark-haired; the black boy was shorter, more compact, with a jaunty kind of gait. Kate wondered what their faces were like. You couldn't tell much from just a backview. Sometimes the owner of a promising back would turn round and give you the shock of your life. Other times –

'– sense of purpose,' said Vanessa.

'What?' Kate was busy trying to skip sideways and make out a profile.

'*Purpose*,' said Vanessa.

She said it rather sternly. Kate nodded and said, 'Right!'

It had been Vanessa's idea to leave Parkhill and transfer to college. She had said it would not only be more mature but that they would mix with a 'more sophisticated type'. Also, the college did a two-year course in Arts and Drama, which Parkhill did not. Arts and drama were very important to Vanessa. Since the age of twelve, when she had seen Laurence Olivier in the film of *Othello*, she had had her future all mapped out: she was going to go to university and get a degree, and then she was going to train to become a director. Ultimately she was going to take over as Head of the National Theatre.

Kate didn't have any such grandiose notions. She sometimes thought she might quite like to be an actress (though not if it meant being directed by Vanessa), but really it had been more a case of what Vanessa suggested, Kate going along with. Not that Kate invariably did what Vanessa suggested. Often she did; but not always. Vanessa, everyone said, was the stronger of the two, but Kate had a mind of her own.

That mind, just at the moment, was devoid of all thoughts save one: it wanted to get round to the front of the two boys and see what they looked like. There hadn't been any boys at Parkhill High: no boys, no men. The Nunnery was how the inmates had referred to it.

'– make such a change,' said Vanessa, 'being treated *responsibly* for once. People being *motivated*. None of that stupid, childish –' She broke off and looked at Kate with some irritation. 'What are you jiggling about for?'

Kate scuttled crabwise towards her. She spoke out of the side of her mouth: 'Trying to see what they look like.'

'What who look like?'

'Them.' Kate nodded, in the direction of the two boys.

Vanessa raised her eyebrows. 'Trottie, you are so *trivial*!'

Kate was indignant. Vanessa was a fine one to talk! She hadn't seemed to think it trivial when they'd been enclosed in the Nunnery. She'd been every bit as anxious as Kate to get out into the world. Kate reminded her of the fact – 'And don't call me Trottie!'

'Sorry,' said Vanessa. 'I forgot.'

'You *promised*.'

'Yes, I know. I'm sorry.'

'Not much good being sorry,' grumbled Kate.

'Look, just shut up! I won't ever call you Trottie again. That's a promise.'

'Oh, yes?'

'*Yes.*'

They had come to the entrance of the students' lounge. The two boys had stopped. They were standing back, waiting for Kate and Vanessa to go through. Kate risked a quick glance. It was so quick (she didn't want to make it *too* obvious) that she really didn't see very much, other than that the black boy was grinning and the other one was holding open the door. Kate gave him her best smile and was about to say 'Thank you' as she swept graciously past – as graciously as one could, being a person of somewhat stunted stature – when he got in ahead of her.

'Are you a Trot?' he said.

This time, she *did* look at him. (What was he talking about? Are you a Trot?) He didn't exactly have the face of a film star; on the other hand, he wasn't too bad-looking. In fact, quite reasonable, really. He had one of those rather thin, narrow faces that indicated cleverness, and regular features of a kind Kate envied. What Vanessa would have called 'oh-so-terribly-English'. Not spectacular enough for Vanessa – she preferred more flamboyant types. But then, Vanessa could afford to be choosy.

'A Trot,' said the boy. 'Short for Trotskyite.'

Kate didn't know what a Trotskyite was. Vanessa evidently did. She gave a great happy peal of laughter and tossed her long, red-gold hair over her shoulders. (Tossing her hair was one of Vanessa's favourite gestures.)

'Trotskyite! She's practically a Fascist!'

'I am not!' Kate was outraged. She knew what a Fascist was, and she certainly wasn't one of those. Vanessa always accused people of being Fascists when they didn't think exactly the same way as she did.

'So why do you call her Trottie?'

Kate sent a furious, silent signal: DON'T YOU DARE! Vanessa, as usual, chose to ignore it.

'Oh, that's because when she was small she used to walk around like this –' Vanessa set off in a circle, trotting up and down, niddy-nodding with her head. 'Trit-trot, trit-trot, just like a little pony.'

There were times when Kate would have liked to throttle Vanessa. The black boy looked at her and winked. Commiserating? She beamed at him, gratefully. (*He* didn't look like a film star, either. Film star's friend, perhaps? He had the sort of wide-apart brown eyes and pugnacious jaw that film star's friends tended to have. He wasn't tall enough to be an actual star, any more than Kate was. She knew this because Vanessa had told her: you have to be *tall*. Vanessa was tall.)

'I take it,' said the first boy, 'that you two already know each other?'

Vanessa gave a short laugh. 'That,' she said, 'is putting it mildly!'

'Her father –' Kate jerked a thumb.

'– married her mother.'

'Which makes us sisters.'

'Sort of.'

Yes, and sometimes it was very sort of. (Such as when Vanessa would persist in calling her Trottie, even though she'd *promised*.) Other times, just now and again, they were as close as real sisters.

'Do you two know each other?' said Kate.

The two boys stepped back a pace. They raked each other up and down.

'Never seen him in my life before!'

She didn't know whether they meant it or

whether they were pulling her leg. That was the trouble with having spent all one's formative years in a nunnery: one just didn't *know*.

The black boy was called Danny – Danny McEvoy. The white boy was Ned Carey.

'I'm Kate,' said Kate, 'and she's Vanessa. We're doing Arts and Drama. What are you?'

The two boys said that they were doing Arts and Drama, too.

'Which group?' Kate scanned the notice board, peering short-sightedly for names. (She had her reading glasses in her bag, but who wanted to wear reading glasses unless they absolutely had to?)

'There,' said Danny. He jabbed a thumb.

'Oh, yes . . . Group A!' Kate turned, enthusiastically, to Vanessa. 'Isn't that nice? We're all in the same group!'

Vanessa arched an eyebrow: a sign of displeasure. They had had all this out the night before, curled side by side on the divan in Kate's bedroom, with Jacko asleep, nose to tail, dreaming of cats, on the pillow. They had solemnly agreed that the way to treat men was to be laid back and cool. They had made a pact, that this was how they would be. Now Kate was breaking the rules before they had even begun.

'Of course,' murmured Ned, 'it could turn out to be quite horrid . . . you could decide you couldn't stand the sight of us.'

Was he laughing at her?

Vanessa flickered her eyes (green, wouldn't you know it? Actual, real *green*) in the direction of the lounge clock. There were ten minutes to go before their first class.

'Coming to look for the washroom?' she said to Kate.

Kate didn't particularly want to look for the

washroom. She would rather have stayed in the lounge and gone on talking to Ned and Danny. But, she supposed, if Vanessa were going, she had better go with her. After all, Ned and Danny mightn't want her to stay and talk to them. They might prefer to be by themselves. You just didn't know with men.

'Honestly!' said Vanessa, as they walked back down the corridor. 'You are so naive!'

Kate hung her head. She knew it to be true. 'Young for your years' old Woodie had said, trying to persuade her to stay on at Parkhill rather than transfer to college. She scurried to keep up with Vanessa, striding long-legged down the corridor ahead of her.

'Do you think they really haven't seen each other before? Or was it a joke?'

'A joke,' said Vanessa. She sounded scornful. Fancy Kate not realizing that! 'They're probably from the same school.'

'They don't *sound* as if they are.'

'Well, I don't expect we do, either.'

'We do,' said Kate. She had a good ear for accents. Their English teacher at the Nunnery had said so. 'We're both south suburban. Danny isn't; he's London. Ned's –'

'Rawl Escot and gahden pahties.' Vanessa pursed her lips and made a quacking sound like a duck: 'Wha wha wha!'

'Well, there you are,' said Kate.

'Doesn't prove anything. Stop being so *trivial* . . . carrying on about the way people speak! What's it matter?'

'I didn't say it mattered. I just –'

'Oh, Trottie, do shut up!'

Kate subsided resentfully into silence. Mutinously she followed Vanessa into the washroom. She stood watching, brooding, dabbling her hands under the hot tap as Vanessa took out a comb and ran it through the thick curtain of her hair. Kate's hair was black and straight, cut short with a fringe. She told herself that she liked short hair, it was so much easier, so much more practical, but the truth was you couldn't wear it hanging round your shoulders when you had a head the size of a pea and a ridiculous little round face with boot-button eyes and a blob for a nose.

Once, ages ago, when she and Vanessa had been having their photographs taken, the man who was taking the photographs had told Kate that her face was 'cheeky'. He had made it sound as if a cheeky face were an asset to be prized. She gazed at herself in the glass over the wash-basins. *Was* it cheeky? Or was it just round?

Vanessa caught her eye. 'Are you sulking?' she said.

'Me?' said Kate. 'What for?'

'Because I went and called you Trottie again . . . I didn't mean it. Truly! It's just that I'm so *used* to calling you Trottie –'

Kate was so used to it, too. She was so used to it that she hadn't even noticed.

'Just don't do it again,' she said.

'I won't!' said Vanessa. 'I promise! Where do we have to go at ten o'clock?'

Kate consulted her timetable. Vanessa's was identical except that sometimes when Kate had a free period, Vanessa had advanced-level history, and in some of Vanessa's free periods Kate was doing a course called *Introduction to Operating Systems, Databases, Spread Sheets and Word Processing*. She hadn't specially wanted to be introduced to any of these things, it was just that everyone had said how useful they would be; meaning how useful for somebody such as Kate who had vague ideas about becoming an actress and no ideas at all about actually earning a living.

'So what have we got?' Vanessa craned over Kate's shoulder. 'Room 4.4 . . . PD.' She looked at Kate: Kate looked back at her. 'What on earth,' said Vanessa, 'is PD?'

2

PD was a mystery. Kate thought there must have been a mistake and that the person who had written it on the master timetable was dyslexic. What it *ought* to say was DP, standing for drama production. Vanessa agreed, but ventured to suggest it was more likely Kate who was dyslexic (being short-sighted and not wearing her reading glasses) and had copied it down wrong. Of course, Vanessa *would* suggest that.

'At least I copied it,' said Kate. 'You just stood around ogling.'

'Me?' said Vanessa. 'I wasn't the one making eyes!'

When they finally located Room 4.4 they found the rest of the group already there and waiting.

'DP?' said Kate.

Five faces turned to stare at her.

'PD,' said Ned.

Kate slammed the door, triumphantly.

'All right,' said Vanessa. 'You don't have to be aggressive about it. What's it supposed to stand for, anyway?'

'Public dissection,' said Ned. 'We're all going to be stripped naked and systematically dismembered . . . metaphorically speaking.'

'Charming!' said Vanessa.

Danny grinned, and patted the empty chair next

to him as an invitation to one of them to sit down. Kate sat. She knew she ought not (cool and laid back) but there were two other girls there, watching, and she couldn't resist the temptation. Vanessa could be cool and laid back if she chose; it wasn't in Kate's nature.

Paul Morrison, who took them for the mysterious PD and was also the Head of the Arts and Drama Department, came as rather a shock. He was young, for a start – about twenty-eight, Kate would have said, though she wasn't too clever at guessing people's ages. (For years she had thought old Woodie must be at least seventy, whereas she'd turned out to be no more than fifty-five.) In addition to being young he had extraordinarily blond, curly hair and piercing blue eyes. Everybody did a double take, including Miss Laid-back Cool herself. ('Failed actor,' she said to Kate later, but Kate didn't believe it. Nobody could fail with looks like that.)

'OK. Right! Let's get down to business.' Mr Morrison (you had to call tutors Mr, didn't you? Even if they were young) pulled up a chair. He wore a ring on his right hand, but not on his left. Not that that was necessarily anything to go by. Men that were married didn't always wear wedding rings. 'I'm Paul Morrison. You can tell me who you are when I'm through doing my bit. For a start, I dare say you're wondering what PD stands for. Any suggestions?'

Ned said, 'Public Dissection.'

'I like it!' Mr Morrison stuck up a thumb. 'Public Dissection . . . yes! There are those who might agree with you. I don't. I don't see it that way. I see it as . . . exploration. Finding out. What some people call self-awareness, what others call discovery through improvization. I call it personal development . . . hence PD. And I'm going to warn you, right here and now, that it's tough. If anyone came on to this course under the impression that it was going to be a soft option, then forget it! I can't speak for my colleagues, but you can take it from me that nobody swans through *my* classes on the strength of a pretty face. Some people can't take it: they're the ones that drop out. But for those that can – well, I can promise you that at the end of two years you'll know yourselves a whole lot better than you do now. A whole lot better than most people ever know themselves. And that is a very useful attribute to have, because believe you me, it's a jungle out there. The more you're aware of what motivates you, the more chance you stand of surviving. Forewarned, as they say, is forearmed. Right?'

Vanessa nodded and said, 'Right!' She sounded very positive about it. Kate was used to Vanessa sounding positive, but the other two girls in the group both turned in silent surprise to look at her.

Kate took the opportunity to study them. One, she supposed, could be said to be quite prettyish, in a rather ephemeral sort of way. She had an air of fragility about her, as if the least puff of a summer breeze would blow her over. She wasn't particularly thin, or even, for that matter, more than averagely slender (Vanessa, later in the day, said scathingly that her bottom was too big . . . 'I can't stand people with big bottoms!' Vanessa was nothing if not intolerant) so perhaps it was something to do with the fact of her hair being very fine and mouse-coloured, and her skin being very pale, like milk without the cream. She was wearing a frilly blouse, all floppy and limp; the kind that grandmothers wore.

The other girl was nondescript. She had nondescript hair, dark and hanging in straggles, a nondescript face, rather sallow, with a long nose, and was wearing the most totally and utterly nondescript clothes. Tweedy skirt and boring sweater. Kate wondered what such a nondescript sort of person was doing on a drama course.

'OK! Let's get started. You!' Mr Morrison shot out a finger, seemingly at random. It came to rest in front of the nondescript girl. 'Come out here and tell us about yourself . . . who you are, what you are, why you are . . . anything that strikes you as significant. Just a few sentences, we don't necessarily want a full-scale biography.'

The nondescript girl said that her name was Sara Miller. She had two sisters and one brother. Her sisters were both at university; her brother was still at school. Both her parents were teachers. Her father was a chemistry teacher, her mother taught languages. Her brother was going to be a molecular biologist – whatever that might be, thought Kate. The Millers, as a family, were obviously stuffed full of brains. A bit like Vanessa, except that Vanessa had *pop*. Sara was really rather wishy-washy. Kate wondered again what someone so nondescript was doing on a drama course.

'Right,' said Mr Morrison. 'Who's next?'

Vanessa was next. She looked at Kate with raised eyebrow. Kate nodded.

'Can we do it together?' said Vanessa.

'Why? Are you a comedy team?'

'No, it's just that her mother –'

'– married her father.'

'Which makes us sisters.'

'Sort of.'

They were skilled at doing their double act. It was something they had perfected over the years.

'I'm Vanessa Bland,' Vanessa would say, 'and she's Kate Cochrane.'

'Cochrane,' Kate would explain, 'was my father's name.'

Even at the age of twelve she hadn't seen why she should have to change her name just because her mother had. She liked the name Cochrane. Of course, as Vanessa never failed to point out, women didn't ever really have names of their own; not in this male-dominated society. Vanessa was very feminist.

When they had finished, Mr Morrison said, 'Ye-e-e-es . . . Cochrane and Bland. Sounds like a music-hall act! I'll let you get away with it this time, but don't think you can always fall back on it. Next!'

The boy who came next was the sort that Kate's mother lived in dread of. He was scruffy, and long haired, and the collar of his shirt had a tide-mark round it. He slouched round-shouldered and pigeon-toed to the centre of the room, slumped himself down on to the chair. His face was harsh and bony, with deep-sunk eyes and a nose that was too prominent, not because it was especially large, as noses went, but because his face was too thin. Kate's mother would have said how plain he was: Kate thought he looked interesting.

'So let's be hearing from you,' said Mr Morrison.

'You want to hear from me? OK.' The boy crossed his feet at the ankles, displaying threadbare patches in the soles of both shoes. Heavy eyelids drooped over his eyes. His voice was slow, almost deliberately drawling. 'My name's Joshua Levy. You can call me Josh. I'm sixteen years old and I come from Canada. My dad works at the Embassy, my mom stops home. I don't know what she does all day 'cos I don't live there any more.'

There was a silence.

'Is that it?' said Mr Morrison. Josh shrugged. 'So be it. I'm not here to interrogate. Next!'

Danny came next. He told them in detail about his family.

'There's my dad; he works on the buses. He's all right. A bit of a nutcase. Does these incredibly inept things like hooking pots of paint on the tops of ladders then forgetting about them and moving the ladders . . . which is why we've got a bright red garden path. 'Cos he forgot the paint and moved the ladder. But he's OK. Then there's my mum. She's ace. She works at the spastics' home up the road. She's really great with all these little spastic kids. Then there's my sister, Joanne. She's a pain. Then there's my other sister, Dale. She's another pain. Then there's Steven. He's my brother. He's thirteen, and he's the biggest pain of the lot. I have to share a bedroom with him. I tell you there's nothing worse than having to share a bedroom with a kid of thirteen. One of these days I'm going to have a place where I can have a room of my own. That is my real immediate aim in life . . . somewhere I can be on my *own*.'

Everybody laughed, but Kate knew how he felt: she had once had to share a bedroom with Vanessa for a whole month, when the family had gone on holiday. It had been horrific.

The girl with the bottom got up. She was called Christine Cooper. She had been acting, she said, since she was five years old (Vanessa jabbed Kate rather violently in the ribs: Kate pressed with her foot against Vanessa's) when she had been chosen to play the part of the Dormouse in a production of *Alice* for a local drama group.

'The Bromley Barnstormers.' (Vanessa gagged.) 'You may have heard of them, they're quite well known. I mean, they're not just rubbish. They do a production every year. Last year it was the *Snow Queen*.' She paused. 'The local paper came.' (*Jab*, went Vanessa's elbow: *crush* went Kate's foot.) 'They said – oh, but I shouldn't tell you really! It sounds like showing off.'

'Feel free,' said Mr Morrison.

'Shall I? Oh, all right! They said I reminded them of the young Greta Garbo.'

There was a long silence; then Mr Morrison said: 'A bit before my time, I'm afraid.' He said it a trifle drily – at least, Kate thought he said it a trifle drily. She certainly hoped he did. If someone who looked like Paul Morrison found a girl who wore frilly blouses anything but a complete turn-off she might as well give up. No power on earth would get Kate into a blouse like that. And who was Greta Garbo, anyway?

'*I wanna be alone*,' husked Ned.

'Thank you, Ms Garbo!' Mr Morrison inclined his head. 'We'll let you know.'

'Was that Garbo?' said Danny. 'I thought she was that other one.'

'What other one?'

'One with the –' Danny made shapes in the air.

'That was Mae West,' said Ned. He leered, lascivious. '*Come up and see me some time . . .*'

'Very good!' said Mr Morrison. 'Are you a female impersonator?'

'Secret transvestite.'

'Well, it takes all sorts . . . one strives to be broad-minded. Out you get!' Mr Morrison crooked a finger. 'Your turn to entertain us.'

Ned was obviously something of a comedian. He could remember his first performance, he said, as if it were yesterday.

'There I was, sitting on my little potty – one year old, the cynosure of all eyes . . . I remember my Great Aunt Harriet was there. I reminded her, she said, of Charles Laughton playing the Hunchback of Notre-Dame.' Ned slouched, slack-mouthed, hunchbacked, on his chair. 'Then there were all the dear old school performances . . . how I shone in *The Importance*! I played the part of Lady Bracknell. *To be born* –' Ned's chest swelled, imperiously. His voice rose half an octave – '*or at any rate bred in a handbag seems to me to display a contempt for the ordinary decencies of family life that reminds one of the worst excesses of the French Revolution. And I presume* –' he fixed Vanessa with a glassy stare – 'I presume you know what THAT unfortunate movement led to?'

Everyone laughed except Vanessa, who tilted her chin, and Mr Morrison, who said, 'All right, all right! Cut the funny stuff. Tell us something important.'

'Something important. Uh . . .' Ned let his chest deflate. 'There's my mother. I suppose she would count as important. She's a writer; writes historical biographies. Wins prizes and things. Very successful lady, my mother.'

'Woman,' said Vanessa.

'Woman,' said Ned. 'If you prefer.'

'Yes, I do prefer! It's –'

'Quiet!' Mr Morrison rapped with the flat of his hand on the desk. 'You can pursue your private ideologies outside. This is *my* time. Now – hands up anyone who's actually thinking of making the theatre their career. Anyone?'

Vanessa's hand shot into the air, beating Christine's by the merest split second. Sara's followed – 'But teaching,' she said, 'not acting.' (That explained it, thought Kate. Those who can, do; those who can't, teach. At least, that was what Vanessa said.) Josh, Danny and Kate all had their arms at half mast, as if not quite decided. Only Ned made no move.

'So!' said Mr Morrison. 'That gives us three would-be Thespians, three may-be Thespians, and one –' He looked at Ned. 'One what?'

'Soldier,' said Ned.

'*Soldier*?' That was Vanessa. She had a thing against the army. (Vanessa had things against all sorts of things.)

Mr Morrison said, 'Shut up! Who pulled your string?' and turned back to Ned. 'That's a pretty unusual choice for a student on a drama course. What made you – ?' He waved a hand.

'PD?' said Ned. 'Personal development?'

'Mm . . .' Slowly, as if considering the idea, Mr Morrison nodded.

'There's more to being a soldier,' said Ned, 'than simply learning how to fire a gun.'

'Mm –'

'I mean . . . soldiers are people.'

'Ha!' From somewhere to Kate's left came a loud snort of derison. Mr Morrison spun round.

'Was that supposed to be a comment?'

'Yes.' Vanessa faced him, boldly.

'Did anyone *ask* for your comments?'

'No, but it's something I feel strongly about.'

'So maybe it's something Ned feels strongly about!'

Ned, almost imperceptibly, shook his head. Watching him, Kate thought it wasn't that he didn't feel strongly; rather that it was something he didn't choose to discuss at this moment in this company. Or at any rate, not with Vanessa. She did *wish* Vanessa wouldn't show them up like this. It was bad enough when she carried on at home, but to do it here, on their very first day –

Vanessa was looking rebellious. 'If we can't express opinions, it's no better than Hitler's Germany.'

'You can express opinions,' said Mr Morrison, 'when I say that you can. Now just take a back seat and let's get on with things!'

Vanessa made a huffing noise. Kate did her best to catch Ned's eye, but for the rest of the class he didn't look in her direction. It was a pity. She would have liked to signal sympathy; let him know that just because she and Vanessa were sisters-sort-of didn't necessarily mean they shared the same prejudices. *She* didn't see anything wrong in Ned becoming a soldier. *She* didn't have things about the armed forces, and religion, and capitalism, and the Government, and just about everything under the sun the way Vanessa did.

She was anxious that it should be known: she, Kate, was her own person, not a clone of Vanessa.

During the lunch break they all went up in a bunch to the refectory (all except Josh, who said that he had things to do. Josh, they were to discover, quite often had 'things to do'. He was a bit of a loner.) Vanessa started in on Ned almost immediately.

'You can't be serious,' she said. 'You can't *really* be going to join that mob?'

Kate thought she saw a spark of something dangerous in Ned's eye. It was there for just a second, and then had gone. His voice as he said, 'To which mob are you referring?' was quite cool and calm; even, almost, bantering.

'That load of semi-automatic morons . . . your wonderful *army*!'

Kate cringed.

Ned said, 'Oh! That mob,' and leaned forward to inspect the contents of his soup bowl. 'This looks remarkably like washing-up water to me . . . old washing-up water strained through a sock.'

'Sock soup,' said Kate.

'Sock consommé.'

'Soupe à la socque.'

'Soupe à la –'

'That's right,' said Vanessa, 'that's right! Evade the issue.' She dug angrily with her fork into the middle of a pile of spaghetti and began twirling. 'Typical! Absolutely typical! Whatever you do, don't *think*.'

'Can't ask people to go round thinking,' said Danny. 'Might damage the brain.'

Vanessa looked at him, interested. Kate could see her trying to work out whose side he was on. Taking advantage of the brief respite she opened her mouth to say something – *any*thing – when Sara, of all unlikely people, forestalled her.

'Didn't anyone at school try to talk you out of it? A girl at our school thought of the army . . . they talked *her* out of it.'

'Really?' said Ned. 'What for?'

'Well –' Sara faltered, but held her ground. She looked at Ned earnestly; apologetically. It's not really the sort of thing – I mean –'

'For someone of *intelligence,*' said Vanessa.

'I mean, there are more . . . *social* sort of things. More –'

'Why pussyfoot?' said Vanessa.

Ned choked into his soup. 'I hadn't noticed that we were!'

'Well, we have been! What she's trying to say is that it's *barbaric*. The whole concept! The *art* –' Vanessa's lip curled – 'the *art* of *warfare* . . . you call that civilized?'

'I don't call it anything. It just happens to be the job I'm going to do.'

'But why?' Sara leaned forward, urgently, across the table. Kate was really surprised at her. She had seemed so dim and retiring.

'Well,' said Ned, 'since you ask –'

'Yes?' said Vanessa. 'Since we ask?'

' 'Twas a curse put upon me . . . when I were but a tiny lad. That old wicked fairy, she waved her magic wand and "Har, har!" she chortled. "I be the spirit of the Great British Army . . . I claim the babe as One of Ours . . ." '

Kate giggled. Vanessa made a noise of disgust.

Sara said, 'I think we're embarrassing him. People always make jokes when they're embarrassed.'

'Especially men,' said Vanessa.

'Yes. They get very worried by anything personal.'

'Anything *emotional*.'

'It scares them.'

'Which is why they prefer to go out and fight.'

Vanessa looked at Ned across the table as she said it, but he didn't take up the challenge and to Kate's relief the conversation moved on, into areas less fraught. Vanessa and Sara retired into their corner to discuss men (about whom, it suddenly seemed, Sara was as much of an expert as Vanessa), Christine seized the opportunity to buttonhole Kate and tell her about the *Snow Queen*, and how the local paper had said she was like Greta Garbo, 'which is daft, of course, because Garbo was something special, I mean she was one of the all-time greats, and me, I'm not anything –'

'Right,' said Kate, with half an ear on what Ned was saying to Danny. ('Did you mean that,' Ned had just said, 'about getting a place of your own?')

'You what?' said Christine.

'What?' said Kate.

'You said –'

'Sorry,' said Kate. 'I –' ('*Mean* it?' said Danny. 'Man, you have to be joking!') – 'wasn't really listening properly –'

'– just that there's a bed going spare in my place if you want it.'

'*Your* place?'

Danny stopped eating. Everyone stopped talking. Vanessa stared.

'You have your own place?'

'Well . . . it's my grandmother's, actually. But she doesn't use it very much. She's in Malta most of the year.'

'And they let you live there on your own?' Kate and Vanessa had suggested to the parents that they should get a place of their own. Kate's mother had said, 'At sixteen? I've never heard of such a thing!' Vanessa's father had said, 'Out of the question. Don't be so ridiculous.'

'You must have very liberated parents,' said Vanessa.

'Well, it was either that,' said Ned, 'or commuting every day from deepest Devonshire.'

'*Devon*shire?'

'Is that where you come from?' said Christine.

'That be where the old ancestral home is.'

'So what on earth made you come here?'

Ned shrugged.

'I mean, Catford,' said Vanessa. 'It's not exactly the hub of the universe.'

'Where were you before?'

'Oh . . . some rat hole.'

'Local?'

Ned shook his head.

'Somewhere in Devonshire?'

'Nope.'

'It must have been a boarding school.'

'Was it a boarding school?'

'Public school?'

'Somewhere famous?'

They looked at him.

'Not particularly,' said Ned.

'But somewhere we'd've heard of?'

'How do I know what you'd have heard of?'

'Eton,' said Kate.

'Harrow,' said Sara.

'That place where they wear dressing gowns –'

'*Dressing* gowns?'

'Blue dressing gowns.'

'No, but seriously,' said Christine.

'Seriously,' said Ned.

'What made you come *here*?'

A faint expression of irritation flickered across Ned's face, and then, as before, was gone.

'Fancied a change,' he said, 'didn't I?'

This time, not even Christine dared pushed him further. There was a pause.

'About this bed,' said Danny.

'Yes. The offer's still open. It's there if you want it.'

'Thing is, man, I'm skint!'

'So? Who's asking for money? If I don't have to shell out, why should you?'

'That is some offer,' said Vanessa.

Ned grinned. 'You want to take it up? You're welcome.'

'Hang about, hang about!' Danny banged on the table. 'She's not the one that's having to share a bedroom!'

'No, but she's prettier than you are, and besides, she might be able to cook.'

Vanessa tossed her head. Kate said, 'She can't cook for toffee!' And even if she could, she wouldn't. Vanessa didn't believe in being anyone's dogsbody.

'Looks like you're stuck with me,' said Danny. 'But it's all right, I make a lovely plate of porridge . . .'

Walking back afterwards to the main study block for double English, Kate found herself next to Danny. For something to say, she said, 'Did you and Ned go to the same school?'

'Me go to the same school as him?' said Danny. 'You out of your tree?'

'I just w –'

I just wondered, she was about to say, where you met. Slowly it dawned on her: they hadn't. Confused and embarrassed she hurried after Vanessa, striding ahead as usual.

'They didn't know each other before!' she hissed.
'Who didn't?' said Vanessa.
'Ned and Danny.'
'So who said they did?'
'You did! You said it was a joke!'
'Said what was a joke?'
'About them saying they'd – oh, never mind! Just forget it.'
Vanessa really was the *end*.

3

'Help!' yelped Kate. 'It's gone eight o'clock!'

'For crying out *loud*!' Vanessa threw her coffee down her throat.

'Don't panic,' said Kate. She tore across the kitchen, caught one foot in Jacko's basket, tripped over Jacko, ended up in a heap by the door. 'If we get a move on we can still make it.'

'Wait for me!' shrieked Vanessa.

From behind his newspaper, Vanessa's father said, 'Do they have to?'

Kate's mother wanted them to finish their breakfast. She pursued them to the door with slices of toast.

'You can't go out without food, it's not good for you.'

They waved her aside, impatiently. (They usually did wave Kate's mother aside.)

'Haven't got time!'

'Got to get the bus!'

'There's more than one bus, and it's better to be five minutes late than go out without eating.'

'Not on a Monday!' wailed Kate.

Monday was indeed a terrible day to start the week. At nine o'clock on the dot, on the *very* dot, in the Torture Chamber (otherwise known as Room 4.4), they had PD with Mr Morrison. He had warned them at the beginning that PD was no soft option;

since then, they had discovered it for themselves. Ned, with some accuracy, labelled it 'a form of group character assassination', but no words in the English language, thought Kate, could be powerful enough to describe the actual stark, paralysing fear that gripped you as you sat there, waiting for the axe to fall. Waiting for Mr Morrison to turn his merciless blue-eyed glare in your direction and say, 'Right! You! Out there and do it!'

It wasn't so much what he gave you to do as the things he said to you after you'd done it. In other circumstances, the exercises he set might have been fun.

'You're a boy and a girl who've been out together for the evening, right? He's just brought her home, she's asked him in for a coffee. Scene is, she's been leading him on all evening but hasn't the least intention of giving it to him. He's just tumbled to it. Yes? Right! You – and you! Out there and do it. And I want *reactions*.'

The first week he had torn strips off Danny for playing the fool and angrily accused Christine of being prissy. Vanessa had thought it quite amusing until the following week, when it had been her turn, and Mr Morrison had sarcastically informed her that if she were always that bitchy with her boyfriends she could think herself lucky she hadn't ended up in a ditch with her throat cut a long time ago. ('Sexist pig!' raged Vanessa.) He'd told Ned that he was like a wet fart, Josh that he was behaving like a homicidal maniac, and Sara that she was in danger of disappearing up her own backside – except that he didn't put it quite as politely as that.

Kate he had let off comparatively lightly, contenting himself with saying that she had been 'too nice by half'. Unfortunately he had added the rider that, 'If that was supposed to be leading him on, then it's about time you went away and learnt a few things about male psychology!' He had said it quite kindly, but still it had made her feel about fourteen years old, especially as everyone had laughed.

This week, it was anybody's guess where the axe would fall.

'Chances are,' panted Vanessa, galloping like a racehorse down the garden path, 'he'll pick on who-ever's last in.'

'That'll be us, for sure.' Kate hurtled frantically in Vanessa's wake. 'I knew we should've gone to bed earlier!'

Half-past midnight it had been. They had spent the evening with Ned and Danny, in Ned's grand-mother's flat in Greenwich. It had got so late they had missed the last train and had had to call a minicab, which they hadn't had the money to pay for. Vanessa's father had had to come downstairs in his dressing gown and settle up for them. He had not been best pleased. (Kate's mother had stood on the top landing wearing her bedtime hairnet saying, 'Oh, you are naughty girls, you really are very naughty girls! I nearly called the police out. Where have you been?' But they didn't very often take much notice of Kate's mother.)

'It was your fault,' said Kate, 'going on arguing.'

Vanessa tossed her head. 'I wasn't arguing! It was him.'

'Yes, but who was he arguing with? You!'

Ned and Vanessa couldn't be together for five minutes without exchanging words. Vanessa said that Ned rubbed her up the wrong way. It could equally well be said, in Kate's view, that Vanessa rubbed Ned up the wrong way. She would keep needling him about the army. Ned, as a rule, managed to keep fairly cool (Vanessa, in contrast, always grew fearsomely and furiously angry). Last night was the closest Kate had seen him come to losing his temper: he had actually shouted. Vanessa, needless to say, had shouted back. They had gone at it until almost midnight. Kate, having long since given up the unequal struggle and gone to sleep, propped against Danny on the hearth rug, had woken reluctantly to find Vanessa tight-lipped and Ned seemingly on the verge of an apoplexy. (Vanessa really *was* going to give somebody a heart attack one of these days.)

They breasted the slope at the top of the road, only to see their bus wallowing half a mile ahead in a sea of traffic.

'That's torn it!' yelled Vanessa.

As Kate had predicted, she and Vanessa were the last to arrive, hot on the heels of Mr Morrison. As Vanessa had predicted, the last in were the two on whom the axe fell.

'You –' A finger shot in their direction. 'You live together. There are times when you get on each other's nerves, right?'

'Right,' said Kate, surprised that he should know.

'Right!' With sinking heart she realized that he didn't: it was another of his scenarios. 'Get up there and give me something. And remember – I want reactions. Yes? Right!'

Vanessa, with a grimace, scraped back her chair. Kate followed, quaking. Danny, catching her eye, gave her a sympathetic wink.

'OK,' said Vanessa, squaring up. Vanessa was never one to waste time. 'So now what's the big whinge?'

That was a mean trick, throwing the ball into Kate's court. Kate seized on the first genuine grievance which came to mind: 'Calling me Trottie,' she said. Vanessa was still doing it, in spite of having promised. Force of habit, she claimed it was. 'I've told you and *told* you.'

'So, all right, so sometimes I forget! I don't do it on purpose.'

'I don't think you even bother to try.'

'Oh, don't be so petty and over-sensitive . . . What's it matter, what people call you?'

'I'd like to hear what you'd say, if I went round calling you Carrot Top! You'd start squealing soon enough!'

'Pick pick pick,' said Vanessa, 'that's all you ever do!'

The scene went on. Kate dredged up every petty accusation she could think of, from Vanessa's habit of slamming doors to her habit of leaving hair all over the bathroom washbasin. Vanessa retaliated with Kate's habit (*she* said) of disappearing 'whenever it's your turn to do the washing-up', and 'slobbering over that mangy ratbag of a dog'.

Kate saw red at that. 'Don't you start having a go at Jacko! He was part of the family when my father was there . . . long before you lot came barging in!'

Vanessa threw her hair back. 'I can assure you,' she said, 'it gave *me* no pleasure, moving to some grotty little semi in suburbia.'

They were treading dangerous ground. Kate, right at the beginning, had resented the intrusion of Vanessa and her father. Vanessa, for her part, had despised both Kate and Kate's mother and their whole way of life, and had taken no trouble to hide the fact. But all that was past and forgotten. Kate wasn't sure that she liked this trawling in muddied waters. Who knew to what depths they might plummet, what hidden hostilities they might stir up, down in the dank dark of their subconscious?

'I think we ought to stop this,' she said. 'I think we're being rather silly.'

'Speak for yourself!' said Vanessa; but she, too,

was obviously scared, for she made no attempt to carry on.

'Is that it?' said Mr Morrison.

Kate looked at him. Wasn't it enough?

'What made you stop?' He addressed the question specifically to Kate.

'I thought it was getting out of hand,' said Kate.

'It was supposed to get out of hand! That was the whole object of the exercise. Why pull back?'

Kate stuck out her lower lip: she could be stubborn when she chose. 'I reckoned it had gone far enough.'

'*You* reckoned it had gone far enough? It's not up to you to reckon! I'll tell you when it's gone far enough – I'll tell you when to stop! When I say I want reactions, I want reactions, and I mean *reactions* – and where the hell have you been?' This as the door opened and Ned appeared. In all the tension of the past few minutes, Kate hadn't realized that he was missing.

'Sorry,' said Ned.

'Sorry? What do you mean, sorry? You're half an hour late!'

'Yeah, I meant to tell you,' said Danny.

'Tell me what?'

Danny looked across at Ned. Kate saw him raise an eyebrow. Ned, very faintly, shook his head.

'Would someone kindly explain to me,' roared Mr Morrison, 'what is going on here?'

'I missed the bus,' said Ned.

'Oh! You missed the bus! You consider that sufficient excuse, do you? You think you can just come breezing in –'

Kate relaxed. She was sorry the pressure was on Ned, but at least if it was on him it meant it wasn't on her.

* * *

On alternate weeks, Group A had classes called Movement–and–Dance and Mime–and–Gesture. Last week it had been Movement and Dance with Larry Gordon, this week it was Mime and Gesture with Miss Audrey. They clustered on the landing outside Studio 1, waiting for the previous class to finish.

'Where's Ned?' said someone.

'Ned is here, never fear –' Ned clumped up the stairs one by one, shoulders slouched, doing his Hunchback of Notre-Dame act. 'When they say gesture –' he straightened up as he reached the top – 'what sort, one wonders, do they mean?'

'This sort?' said Danny.

Kate giggled. She was starting to get used to Danny.

Christine said, 'Do we have to?'

Ned and Danny exchanged faces.

'Sorry, I'm sure,' said Ned. He coughed. 'I really must stop smoking.'

'But you don't!' said Kate.

Ned coughed again. 'No, I don't,' he said. 'Full marks . . . you noticed!'

Kate looked at him in bewilderment. She was getting used to Danny, but there were times when she still didn't understand Ned. He winked at her, and ruffled her hair. (He wouldn't have *dared* do that to Vanessa.)

'Don't worry,' he said. 'It's not catching.'

Miss Audrey, a small, sharp-faced, spidery woman dressed in pink chiffon trousers and a sparkly top, with orange hair and fingernails to match, was not one for any horseplay. She kept Ned and Danny very firmly in their place by quellingly addressing them as 'young man' in tones which succeeded in reducing them to the level of first formers.

'I will not have smut,' she said. 'Smut is for children. We are not children here, we are young adults.

Let us endeavour to behave as such – and you can stop that smirking, young man! It does not become you.'

They spent most of the class unpacking imaginary suitcases and taking out imaginary objects which the others had to identify – 'We will have no undergarments,' said Miss Audrey. 'Neither of the male variety nor the female' – and in learning how to do a special mime walk, walking on the spot. Everybody was hopeless at it save Kate and Danny. Kate was so busy gloating over the fact of being able, for once, to do something better than Vanessa (Vanessa looked like nothing so much as a spastic ostrich having an epileptic fit) that she didn't immediately realize Miss Audrey was beckoning her and Danny to 'come out the front and demonstrate'.

'You! The little girl with the freckles –'

'Trottie,' said Ned.

Kate spun round.

'Trottie, is it? Come along then, Trottie!' Miss Audrey crooked a finger. 'Don't be shy!'

'Off you go, Trottie!' Ned gave her a little push. 'Don't be shy . . .'

'I'll get you for that!' hissed Kate.

Ned just blew her a kiss. (He wouldn't do that to Vanessa, either . . .)

Later in the day, Vanessa had an A level history class while Kate had a free period. Free periods, officially, were known as study sessions. There were special places throughout the building designated 'study areas' where students were supposed to go and sit, where indeed some students, Christine and Sara for example, actually *did* go and sit. Kate usually went to the lounge. She was in there now, scanning the notice board in search of interesting notices, when a hand slid over her shoulder, cupping her breast, and a voice in her ear said, 'Ooh, I feel a right tit!'

The voice belonged to Danny.

'Hang off, dog!' Kate slapped his hand away. (She couldn't help being just a tiny bit pleased with herself. If Danny had done that two weeks ago she would have blushed bright scarlet. It didn't bother her now. She was learning about men.) She turned, and pushed at him. 'Stop being so sexist!'

'What's sexist?' said Danny. 'You can feel my tits any day . . . I've probably got more to feel than you have!'

'Do you mind?' said Kate.

'Not really,' said Danny. 'I quite go for scrawny women.'

Kate battered at him with her duffel bag. 'Where's Ned?'

'Where's Ned? Ned's in bed! What does he wear? HOT PANTS!'

'Shut up!' said Kate. 'Where is he?'

'Doing his hist'ry.'

'Oh?' She hadn't known Ned did history; Vanessa hadn't mentioned it. She frowned, rubbing a finger across her forehead, beneath her fringe. She wondered why Vanessa hadn't said anything.

'What d'you want him for, anyway?' said Danny. 'Aren't I good enough?'

'Not when you behave in that piglike fashion!'

'I bet you wouldn't think it piglike if Nedward did it!'

This time, Kate did blush. 'Ned wouldn't,' she said.

She knew he could fool around, she'd heard him and Danny telling jokes that would have made old Woodie fall off her perch, but he never got fresh with people. Ned had the sort of manners that Kate's mother always said the young men these days weren't brought up to. 'Nobody holds a door for you these days. Nobody stands back to let you pass.' Ned did. Vanessa was scornful. She said that Ned was the 'last bastion of male chauvinism'. Kate, secretly, rather enjoyed it. She thought it was a pity that men didn't still wear hats. She was sure that if they did, Ned would politely raise his and say 'good-morning'.

'Don't you kid yourself,' said Danny. 'These types that go to posh schools, they're the worst of all . . . Why d'you suppose he was so late this morning?'

'I don't know,' said Kate. Now she came to think about it, she did rather wonder. All that eyebrow-twitching and shaking of heads. 'Why *was* he so late this morning?'

' 'Cos it was the night of the full moon . . . Come the witching hour he turns into this sex beast . . . puts on his rubber gloves and his leather gear and goes out on the streets, looking for thrills.'

'Oh, shut up!' said Kate. She biffed at him again with her bag. 'You are so *disgusting*.'

Danny grinned. 'I know,' he said. 'It's part of my charm . . .'

During the lunch break someone from Group B came up and said, 'Is one of you called Trottie? Miss Audrey said you could show us how to do the mime walk.'

Kate looked across, rather hard, at Ned. Ned looked back at her, his gaze bland and innocent. Vanessa meanwhile, without so much as a moment's pause for thought, jerked her thumb in Kate's direction.

'She is,' she said.

'Looks like you're stuck with it,' murmured Danny.

First class of the afternoon was Fencing, which they had together with Group B. Group B, on the whole, didn't strike Kate as being as interesting as Group A.

The only two who really stood out were an immensely large Israeli boy called Asher Zindel, and a girl called Judy Wilson. Everyone knew Judy Wilson. She was the smallest, tubbiest person in the whole college. If Kate had been that size and shape she would have suffered agonies of inferiority, but Judy didn't seem to care. She was very extrovert.

Fencing was taken by Miss Dando, a rather muscular woman whom Ned referred to as 'Dykie Dando'. Kate thought it quite funny, but it sent Vanessa into paroxysms of rage. Another thing that sent her into paroxysms was his nickname of Gay Gordon for Larry Gordon, the Movement teacher. She said that Ned was the 'ultimate sexist creep'. It was strange she never seemed to get mad at Danny, even though (in Kate's opinion) he was even more outrageous than Ned. There was just something about Ned that got her going.

That afternoon, in Fencing, Miss Dando said that now they had learnt how to stand in the on-guard position and had mastered a few simple passes (predictable jokes from male members of the class, instantly quashed by Miss Dando) they could each take a partner and 'Wearing your masks, everybody, please' could have a few practice runs.

'And that includes you, Ned! What are you doing, slumped there? Jump to it!'

Ned, who had taken up residence on the window seat, pulled a face. 'Do I have to?'

'Yes, you do have to! What's the matter with you?'

Everybody turned to look at Ned, sitting on the window seat. He made a gesture, vague and half-hearted.

'It's been a long day.'

'Long day! At your age! Don't be so feeble!' Miss Dando took him by the arm and pulled him to his feet. 'Get out there and find yourself a partner!'

'I'll partner him,' said Vanessa.

Vanessa? Was she *mad*? She and Ned couldn't even sit down to eat lunch together without coming to blows.

For the next few minutes Kate was too busy thrusting and parrying, trying to score points off Danny, to take much notice of what the rest of the class were up to. But every now and again, out of the corner of her eye, she became vaguely aware of hectically slashing swords somewhere away to her right, where Ned and Vanessa had taken up their pitch. The slashing was periodically punctuated by angry cries of pain and anguish, mainly coming from Ned.

'Ow!' Clang. 'These are supposed to be fencing foils, not flaming battleaxes!' Slash. Clatter. 'Listen, you maniac!' Bang. Crash. 'Are you trying to castrate me, or –' Thud. Wallop. 'Or what?' screamed Ned.

Miss Dando's voice, loud and authoritative, cut across the stream of vituperation: 'Right! That's it! That's enough!' (Kate thought, I knew it would end in tears . . .) 'Break it up, you two! Find yourselves new partners – change with the couple on your left.'

The couple on their left were Kate and Danny. For a moment Kate thought Ned might be going to choose her, but then, to everyone's astonishment, he said, 'I really don't feel like doing any more fencing today' and walked out of the room. There was a shocked silence.

'All right,' said Miss Dando. 'Let him go. Vanessa, you'd better partner me.'

Extraordinary! thought Kate. Extraordinary that Ned should dare to just walk out; even more extraordinary that Miss Dando should accept it so calmly. If such a thing had ever occurred at the Nunnery there would have been scandal and repercussions right up as far as old Woodie.

'What I don't understand,' said Kate, as she and

Vanessa changed together afterwards in the girls' cloakroom, 'is what you wanted to go and partner him for in the first place!'

'I thought it might be a challenge,' said Vanessa. 'I hadn't realized he was quite *that* useless. And hot lips and hell fire!' she added. 'It's Duologues next and I've got him again!'

Duologues, presided over by the amiable and mop-headed Michael Burge, were scenes that they had been given to work on in class (to be acted out at half-term before the staff of the Drama Department). The scenes for Group A had been taken from Tennessee Williams' *A Streetcar Named Desire*. To Vanessa's disgust, she had been paired with Ned. Kate thought it was probably to Ned's disgust, too. After the debacle in Fencing she wouldn't have been at all surprised if he had stayed away, but he was already sitting there, script in hand, as the rest of them turned up.

'Fancy seeing you here,' said Vanessa.

'Do you come here often?' said Ned.

'No more than I can help.'

'We really must stop meeting like this!'

'Suits me,' said Vanessa.

It was unfortunate, given the events which had just occurred, that Mr Burge should choose to start straight in on Ned and Vanessa's scene. Even apart from the misery of having to act opposite Vanessa, Ned wasn't exactly having a happy time with *Streetcar*. Everybody (except for Josh) was having difficulty with the accent, but Mr Burge had told them right at the beginning that the accent wasn't important. 'If it comes, it comes; if it doesn't, it doesn't. What I'm more interested in is getting the emotion right.'

Unfortunately, Ned didn't seem able to get that, either.

'No, no, *no*!' Mr Burge clutched his head, as if in agony. 'It's too *nice*! It's too *nice*! This man is a bull – just one big ugly chunk of muscle. Give it some stick, let yourself go!'

Ned couldn't. Kate could see that he couldn't. It was almost as if there were a barrier which came down at a certain point and actually, physically, stopped him. They played the scene three times, each time worse than the time before. Mr Morrison would have lost his temper. Mr Burge just ran his hand through his hair, looked at his watch, and rather wearily said, 'OK. Let's leave it,' which in many ways was even worse. At least if someone lost their temper you felt they hadn't completely given up on you.

Vanessa railed about it all the way home. Ned was impossible; Ned was an idiot. Ned was like a piece of wet flannel. How could she be expected to give anything if he was just going to stand there bleating at her?

'Stanley isn't really his sort of part,' said Kate.

'So it needn't stop him trying. It hasn't stopped Danny. Imagine how *he* feels, having to play Mitch.'

Kate hadn't really given very much thought to Danny having to play Mitch. It seemed to her that he was far more suited to Mitch than Ned was to Stanley.

'You must be joking!' said Vanessa.

'Why?'

Vanessa looked at her. 'The Deep South?'

'Oh! You're just talking about colour. That's not important.'

'It might be to Danny.'

' 'Course it's not! That sort of thing doesn't bother him.' Not Danny, he was far too happy-go-lucky. 'Ned's different. He's just not *right* for Stanley.'

'You mean he just won't try! Too scared of losing his precious dignity. What that guy needs,' said Vanessa, 'is a *rocket* put under him!'

4

'When I say I want emotions, I want emotions!' Mr Morrison glared round the class. 'Right?'

'Right.'

Seven heads nodded, in more or less earnest agreement.

'Very well!'

There was a pause, a moment's respite. Kate let out her breath. Christine, sitting opposite, beamed brightly. What was she beaming for? Fatuous nincompoop! She hadn't beamed last week, when she'd been told she was behaving like a prurient virgin locked up in a brothel. Sexist, Vanessa had said it was; a very sexist remark. A very –

'So!'

Fear, abruptly, descended. Christine stopped beaming, Sara studied the floor. Kate sat rigid, hands clawing the sides of the chair. Danny, next to her, pressed his foot against hers: Vanessa, on the other side, tossed back her hair. Ned coughed.

'Two boys,' said Mr Morrison.

Boys! Oh, relief!

'Both after the same girl.'

GIRL?????????

'You – Edward! – reckon that she belongs to you. And you – Daniel! – reckon she was yours before she was his. Yes?' Kate relaxed. 'Right! *Emotion*. Get on with it.'

Danny, ever willing once the axe had actually fallen, bounced himself into the middle of the room. Ned followed, looking martyred.

'So what's all this –' Danny, like Vanessa, believed in jumping in feet first – 'about you going out with my bird?'

'Bird?' said Ned. 'Are you an ornithologist?'

'Look, don't try the funny stuff, man . . . you were seen! Down the disco, last night. With Julie. Am I right?'

'Oh, with *Julie,*' said Ned. 'Why didn't you say so? When people speak of birds, I always take them to mean the feathered variety. The appellation bird is very much frowned on in feminist circles – or so my feminist acquaintances inform me.'

'Quite right!' said Vanessa.

Ned turned, and bowed. 'I thank you, madam. Your gesture of solidarity is greatly appreciated.'

'Look, just cut the rabbit, OK?'

'When you say, cut the rabbit –'

Halfway through, the scene broke down. It wasn't Danny's fault; he did his best. Ned simply refused to be shaken out of his pose of calm superiority.

'Look, mush –' Danny said it for the third time. There was a growing note of desperation in his voice: help me, or I shall collapse . . . 'She was my bloody bird before she was yours, right?'

'I don't think one should be possessive in these matters. I don't think women like to be spoken of as if they were chattels.'

'I'm not speaking of her as if she were a chattel, I'm just saying that she was my bloody bird before she was yours!'

Ned yawned. 'So if she was your bloody bird, take her back again . . . I didn't particularly go for her, anyway.'

Danny collapsed. So did everyone else. Everyone,

that is, except Mr Morrison. Mr Morrison exploded.

'What the hell is the matter with you? Call that emotion? You're like a wet fish on a slab! God help any woman that goes out with you, if that's all the enthusiasm you can muster!'

'She wasn't really the sort of woman,' mused Ned, 'who rouses enthusiasm . . . she had these great buck teeth and her eyes were crossed. Weren't they?'

He appealed to Danny for confirmation.

'Not when she was my bird they weren't,' said Danny.

'Rat fink!'

Kate wondered how they dared, in front of Mr Morrison. He was plainly not amused.

'What do you think this is? Comedy half-hour? You!' He addressed himself to Ned. 'You're attending this class for one purpose: to stretch yourself to the furthest extent possible. That is *not* going to be achieved by taking the easy way out of every situation. What's your problem? Are you scared of emotion?'

For the first time, Ned seemed uncomfortable. He hunched a shoulder.

'I just don't see there's anything to be gained from losing one's temper.'

'What the devil has that to do with it? This is supposed to be a drama course! Not all the characters you play are going to be cardboard cut-outs of some spineless freak who gives up his girlfriends at the drop of a hat rather than put himself into a bit of a lather by fighting for them!'

Ned flushed. 'I hadn't realized I was supposed to be playing a character . . . I thought I was supposed to be playing me.'

'Don't give me that smart-aleck stuff! Nobody's interested in you playing you. After that performance? You must be joking! What I'm interested in is personal development. Look into yourself – discover what's there. Then utilize it. And don't tell me there isn't any anger in you, because a person without anger is a person that's only half alive; and a person that's only half alive has no damned right to be here! You just remember that. Next time I want a bit of blood and guts . . . none of this wishy-washy *I'm too much of a gentleman to lose my temper* stuff. I want the real thing. Got it? Right. I don't intend to tell you twice. Sit down.'

There was silence as Ned walked to his seat. Kate tried, as she had tried once before, to catch his eye; but as before, Ned wasn't looking. Carefully he avoided looking at anyone. There are some people, Mr Morrison had said, who can't take it: they're the ones that drop out. Kate wasn't at all sure that she would be able to take it. If Mr Morrison were ever to speak to her as he had just spoken to Ned, she thought that she would want to run away and die.

It was not Ned's day. First he was torn to pieces by Mr Morrison. Later, in Speech and Voice, he was put through it by Miss Truscott.

Miss Truscott had once been at RADA and never let anyone forget it. She stalked imperious on six-inch heels, in black crêpe and silver lamé, with her spectacles slung round her neck on a chain. She was very theatrical. Kate, secretly, rather admired her. She thought that when she was Miss Truscott's age, which must be at least sixty, she would like to go round in black crêpe and silver lamé, looking dramatic with her lips bright scarlet and her eyelashes spiky stiff like corkscrews with mascara. There was a certain mad grandeur about it. Better, at any rate, than being a shapeless heap in old grey cardigans and baggy shirts. Even Vanessa said grudgingly that she had a certain something. Ned and Danny called her old Aggie Tosspot and went round mimicking her –

'When I was at *Rah*-Dah' – but even they were always respectful to her face. Not even Ned would have dared cheek Miss Truscott.

The nearest he came to it was that afternoon in Voice. For some reason, they were a chair short in the studio.

'Doesn't matter,' said Danny. 'Trottie can sit on my lap.' (They all called her Trottie now. She had almost given up bothering to protest.)

He had just pulled her down, to the accompaniment of much giggling and squeaking on Kate's part, when Miss Truscott walked in. She raised her spectacles on the end of their chain.

'Hm!' she said.

Kate, blushing, wriggled to her feet.

'There's nowhere else for her to sit,' said Danny.

'Indeed?' Miss Truscott let fall her spectacles. 'Since when has there been a dearth of chairs in this establishment?'

'It's not RADA,' said Ned.

Two hot dabs of colour appeared high up on Miss Truscott's cheeks.

'I am very well aware of *that*,' said Miss Truscott. 'At RADA, the boys would have given up their seats – or have gone and fetched another one.'

Ned took the hint; a chair was brought in from the studio next door and the class began. They started, as usual, with voice exercises – mummymummymummymummymummymummy ninnyninnyninnyninnyninny – then moved on to special sentences for vowel sounds. Today it was 'Witty Kitty McQuitty', and 'On the Strand at Clacton'.

'One by one, if you please,' said Miss Truscott. 'Witty Kitty . . . let us start at this end and work our way round the room.'

Sara was the first to read, Ned, the last. Ned had

hardly even begun before Miss Truscott stopped him.

'Wittay? Kittay? What language, pray, are you speaking?'

Vanessa made a snorting sound. Ned pulled a face.

'I'd thought it was English.'

'Oh, had you? Well, it doesn't bear any resemblance to English as I know it! A most horrible sound . . . Wittay Kittay McQuittay . . .' Miss Truscott curled her lip, disdainfully, as she formed the words. 'Are you related to royalty by any chance?'

'Not as far as I'm aware,' said Ned.

'In that case, kindly remove the plum from your mouth and relax those vowels!'

Christine stifled a giggle. The class continued. Ned, with much dramatic rolling of the eyes from Miss Truscott, staggered through the remainder of 'Witty Kitty'. Sara picked up again with 'On the Strand at Clacton'. Slowly, they worked their way back to Ned. This time, Miss Truscott allowed him to get almost to the end. He had just reached 'plaid plastics for Macbeth' when her voice came booming:

'Pled plestics? Pled plestics? What, pray, are pled plastics? Dear boy, you sound like a demented duck . . . qweck, qweck, qweck! Qwark, qwark, qwark!' Miss Truscott threw her head in the air and trumpeted dramatically. Christine hiccuped, Vanessa gave another snort. 'Hwah, hwah, hwah!' bleated Miss Truscott, enjoying herself. 'Whay don't we all go orff end play a rind of goff? Whah? whah? Sorray? Whah?'

Everybody, by now, was helpless with giggles, even Kate, who hadn't wanted to laugh, because after all Ned couldn't help how he spoke any more than the rest of them could. Miss Truscott was taking a mean revenge. But it *was* funny.

'Where, might one ask,' said Miss Truscott,

abandoning her animal noises, 'have you been educated? Malvern Ladies' College? Some select seminary –' she hung contemptuously upon the word, splitting it into four – 'in S.W.1? Where?'

Ned met her gaze. 'Nowhere particularly special.'

'Nowhere particularly special . . . Well, wherever it was, it's wrought havoc with your vocal apparatus! It's a wonder you haven't strangulated yourself long since. I most sincerely trust you are not contemplating a career upon the boards?'

'Shouldn't dream of it,' said Ned.

'He's going into the *army*.' Vanessa never could resist the temptation to shove her oar in.

'The army?' Miss Truscott elevated both eyebrows so high that her glasses slid to the end of her nose. For a long, disdainful moment she regarded Ned over the top of them. 'How utterly extraordinary!' she said.

Between Voice and the double period of English which ended the day, they had a fifteen-minute break. Group B were in the refectory, loudly bewailing the fact to anyone who would listen – not that it was really possible to avoid it – that Mr Morrison was a sadist.

'Well, we all know *that*,' said Vanessa.

'Tell us something new,' said Kate.

'What's he done now?'

Asher shook his head. 'The man is a pig.'

'Poor pigs,' said someone. 'What have pigs ever done?'

'What has *Morrison* done?'

What Mr Morrison had done, it seemed, was tell Asher that he was a drivelling imbecile, Judy that she had better set about losing some of her flab before she started to look like an ambulatory hovercraft, and a quiet, inoffensive girl whose name Kate could never remember – sometimes she thought it was Marcia, sometimes she thought it was Margaret – that she had no personality and couldn't say boo to her own shadow. Marcia (or Margaret) was now in the girls' cloak-room, weeping.

'Weeping?' said Vanessa. 'What's she weeping for?'

Asher glared. 'Would you like to be told such a thing?'

Kate giggled at the thought of anyone, even Mr Morrison, daring to accuse Vanessa of having no personality. Vanessa, with an impatient gesture, flicked her hair back over her shoulders.

'I wouldn't go away and *weep*!'

'So maybe you're not a very feminine sort of person.'

'Oh, crap!' said Vanessa. 'Masculine, feminine . . . what's with all this sexist rubbish?'

Asher looked affronted. Christine, always eager to jump in on other people's behalf, even when they would rather she didn't, called out across the room to Ned: 'Mr Morrison was absolutely vile to Ned this morning, wasn't he, Ned?'

'Oh! Absolutely atrocious,' said Ned; but Kate noticed that he volunteered no further information and for the rest of the break remained silent, standing to one side and drinking his coffee as the talk swirled round him. It was unlike Ned not to participate; as a rule he was very well to the forefront of any conversation (or more likely conversations) that might be taking place. Kate wished there was something she could say to cheer him up.

He left the refectory ahead of the others. Greatly daring, Kate tossed her cup into the waste bin and hurried after him.

'Are you off to English?'

'Either that or putting a noose round my neck and

throwing myself in the nearest puddle . . . I haven't quite decided.'

There was a silence. Kate racked her brains for something cheerful.

'Did you hear what Mr Morrison said to Asher?' It wasn't exactly cheerful, but at least it might make him feel that he was not the only one.

'No,' said Ned. 'What did Mr Morrison say to Asher?'

'He said he was a drivelling imbecile.'

'Charming.'

'And he told Judy she looked like an ambulatory hovercraft.'

'Even more charming.'

'It's not very nice, is it? I don't see why he had to be insulting.'

'He's only doing his job. It's nothing personal.'

'It sounds pretty personal to me.'

'Yes. Well –' Ned slung his jacket over his shoulder, dangling it by the loop from one finger. 'The guy probably had a rough night. It happens.'

They walked on for a while without speaking.

'Do you like horror films?' said Kate.

'Wild about 'em!'

'Have you ever seen one called *Monster on the M1*?'

Ned said no, he couldn't say that he had.

'It's on this week at Bromley,' said Kate. 'I wanted to go, but Vanessa won't. She says horror films are sexist and moronic.'

'That sounds like Vanessa.'

'I suppose –' Kate hesitated. 'I suppose Bromley's a bit too far for you? Otherwise you could have gone.'

'I'll come with you if you want,' said Ned.

'Oh!' She blushed. 'I didn't mean –'

'Tonight?' said Ned.

'All right!' Kate beamed. Why not?

'Going to the cinema?' Vanessa said it almost accusingly. 'With *Ned*?'

Kate bristled. 'What's wrong with going to the cinema with Ned?'

'Nothing, I suppose, if that's what turns you on.' Vanessa sprang off the bus ahead of Kate and barged her way somewhat huffily through the waiting throng. 'This hole goes from bad to worse! I can't wait to get out – get a place of my *own*.'

'Place of *our* own,' said Kate, hurrying to catch up.

'Yes, if you don't go getting cold feet at the last minute. I know what you're like . . . all mouth and no action. Why didn't you ask Danny? Then we could all have gone.'

She didn't want to ask Danny. She didn't want them all to go. She wanted it to be just her and Ned.

'Anyway,' she said, 'it's *Monster on the M1*. You said wild horses wouldn't drag you to it.'

'No, they wouldn't! Load of rubbish. Why don't we go to the new Ken Russell?'

'Because Ned wants to see *Monster on the M1*.'

'I bet he doesn't! I bet it was your idea. I bet he'd far rather see the Ken Russell.'

'Look, if you want to see the Ken Russell, go and see it! Ring Danny. I'm going to see *Monster on the M1* and I'm going to see it with Ned.'

She didn't see why Vanessa should expect to come shoving in. One didn't want to do *every*thing with Vanessa.

She had arranged to meet Ned at the cinema at quarter to eight. Her mother came fussing after her to the front door.

'You make sure you're home before midnight. I won't have you girls staying out late like this! Just because you're no longer at school . . . you're still only sixteen. When I was sixteen I was expected to be in by ten o'clock. I wasn't allowed to go rampaging about with every Tom, Dick and Harry. My parents were very strict with me.'

Sometimes, to hear Kate's mother talk, you'd think she'd been born at the turn of the century.

Kate had to wait nearly twenty minutes for the bus into Bromley. (Her mother always said that if you left in good time, it wouldn't matter having to wait. Kate's mother always allowed at least half an hour for emergencies.) Ned had already arrived. He was standing outside the cinema, looking at the stills. He had the collar of his jacket turned up, even though it was a warm evening. Kate really loved it, the way he turned up his collar like that; it was really sexy.

'Ah, there you are!' he said.

'Yes, I'm sorry, the b –'

'Don't worry,' said Ned. 'I only just got here myself.'

'Oh.' She immediately felt flattened, though really it was quite illogical. After all, if she could be late why couldn't he?

Monster on the M1 was a fearsome film. It terrified the life out of Kate. The monster was a raving madman who roamed the motorway late at night, flagging down lone lady motorists with red flags and cries of 'Pile-up ahead!' and then, when he'd flagged them down, getting into the car and forcing them to drive at gunpoint about the countryside until they reached a suitable spot where he could satisfy his unnatural desires, which he mainly did by strangling with stockings and hacking with a meat cleaver (which he kept concealed about his person for just such purposes). Vanessa would have said scornfully, 'I told you it would be sexist and moronic.' It was, of course, but that didn't stop the palms of

Kate's hands from sweating or her heart pounding nineteen to the dozen with fear.

Ned coughed occasionally, but otherwise seemed totally unmoved. If Danny had been there he would have put an arm round her or held her hand, but Ned wasn't like Danny. For all his careless banter, Ned was really quite self-contained.

As they left the cinema he said, 'Well! That was jolly, wasn't it? Who knows what one might not meet on a dark night . . . What do you want to do now? Shall we have a coffee?'

'Yes, please!' said Kate.

They didn't sit long over coffee. Ned had to get back to Greenwich, and Kate found herself unexpectedly shy in his company. She wasn't as a rule tongue-tied, but this was the first time she had really been on her own with Ned and she couldn't think what to talk about. Away from college, away from the others, he suddenly seemed so much older. She was scared he might think her immature, that the things she would normally talk about would bore him. Just for a moment, as silence fell between them, she wished that Danny and Vanessa were there; there was never any silence with those two around.

Ned pushed back his chair. 'I'll see you home.'

Confused, Kate said, 'You don't have to.' She didn't want to drag him miles out of his way. Bad enough he should think her immature, she wouldn't want to be thought a nuisance as well. 'I've only got to jump on a bus. There isn't any need for you to come . . . honestly!'

'I can't help it,' said Ned. 'It's the way I'm programmed . . . the circuitry would blow if I behaved out of character. You know,' he said, 'that I am the last bastion of male chauvinism . . . the Harridan says so. Which is your bus stop?'

The bus, fortunately, came almost at once. From

their seat on the top deck Kate pointed out the objects of local interest. 'That's the Town Hall . . . that's the theatre . . . that's our old school.' *Parkhill High School for Girls. Headmistress: Margaret Woodford, MA*. 'Gruesome, isn't it?'

Ned spared it a quick glance. 'Looks OK.'

'We called it the Nunnery. It was dire.' She didn't know why she said that. She had actually quite enjoyed her time at Parkhill. It had been Vanessa who thought it dire, not Kate. She turned from the window to look at Ned. 'Where did you go?'

'Oh, now, come on!' said Ned. 'Don't you start!'

'I was just interested,' said Kate.

'It seems that everyone is just interested. *Consumed with vulgar curiosity* I'd call it. I wasn't thrown out, if that's what you're thinking.'

It hadn't been what she was thinking. As a matter of fact, it hadn't even occurred to her.

She fell silent again, watching through the window as the familiar landmarks loomed up. Kate had lived in the same town, in the same road, in the same house, all her life.

'That's where Vanessa's father works.' She pointed to a modern office block, all flashing glass and stainless steel. 'It's an insurance company. He's an actuary. What's yours?'

'Nothing, now,' said Ned. There was a pause, then he added: 'He's dead.'

'Really?' said Kate. She waited a second. 'So's mine.'

Kate's father had died when she was eight. Vanessa, waspishly, in the early days, when she and Kate had still been resentful of their changed circumstances, had suggested that 'he probably died of boredom'. Actually, it had been a heart attack.

Kate explained this to Ned, thinking that he in turn would tell her about his father, but all he said was: 'How come Vanessa wound up living with you? I thought girls usually stayed with their mothers.'

'She did, for a bit, when they were first divorced. But her mother's a model – well, sort of. I mean –'

Kate struggled for a moment with her conscience, trying to be fair. She had once felt – or at any rate, persuaded herself that she felt – immeasurably superior to Vanessa in this matter of mothers. After all, *she* had one who loved her and cherished her and generally behaved as a mother ought. Vanessa had one who Chased After Men and packed her daughter off like an unwanted parcel the minute she became inconvenient. But just lately, just once or twice, feelings of another kind had begun to creep in. Impatience, perhaps; dissatisfaction. There might be something to be said for having a mother who lived a bit dangerously.

'A *kind* of model. Not medical. I don't think she'd ever do medical. More sort of . . . glamour, with a bit of fashion when she can get it.'

Ned was staring at Kate as one entranced. 'Fashion when she can get it?'

'Front cover of *Vogue*; that sort of thing. But mostly it's just sitting around on car bonnets advertising under-wear.'

'So what's medical? Sitting around on bedpans advertising condoms?'

'Oh, you know!' Kate lowered her voice. 'Without clothes . . .'

'Ah! Like in *Playboy*.'

'Worse than *Playboy*. *Playboy's* glamour. Medical's what you find all torn up and scattered over the common . . . at least, you do over our common.'

'Really?' Ned sounded enraptured. 'The things one learns! You'll have to take me there some time.'

She wondered if he meant it, or whether he was joking. Sometimes, even now, she found it difficult to tell.

Ned left her, chastely, at the front gate. She hadn't really expected him to kiss her – well, she had hoped that he might, but had known that he probably wouldn't, so she wasn't exactly disappointed. Of course it would have been nice if he had, but maybe as it was the first time – maybe if they *did* go over the common – but most likely he was only joking.

She found Vanessa hovering on the upstairs landing.

'You're back early!'

Kate stiffened. Was there just a tiny note of triumph in Vanessa's voice?

'Did you enjoy it?'

'Yes, thank you.'

'I suppose it had lots of blood and gore and screaming women?'

'It was good,' said Kate.

'I notice it didn't exactly fill our Edward with mad passionate rapture . . . Didn't hang about, did he?'

Kate drew herself up. Just what did she mean by that remark?

'I saw you coming down the road,' said Vanessa. 'I thought we'd be in for at least a twenty-minute cuddling session beneath the street lamp.'

Kate flushed, angrily.

'You're like some horrible old woman . . . *spying* on people!'

'I wasn't spying, you stupid cow! What would I want to spy on you for? You think I care what you get up to?' Vanessa tossed her head. 'I've got far better things to do with my time!'

'Pity you don't go and do them!'

'Listen, you s –'

'Girls, girls!' Kate's mother had appeared at the foot of the stairs. 'What are you shouting about?'

'I do not like being *spied* on,' said Kate.

'I wasn't *spying*,' said Vanessa. 'I just happened to

be looking out of the window . . . I suppose a person can look out of the window if a person wants?'

Vanessa marched off across the landing. Kate flounced into her bedroom and banged the door. She heard her mother's voice, plaintive up the stairs: 'Oh, you girls . . . what *am* I to do with you?'

5

'. . . never *known* anybody be so useless. Never *known* anybody –' Just in time, Vanessa hauled her briefcase out of the way. The bus had reached the first stop in the High Street and the usual crowds of school kids were stampeding up the stairs. '. . . anyone that's not a complete *zombie*, which of course, for all I know, he may very well be, the way he carries on . . . You'd think it was a play about non-communication. It's like acting opposite a brick *wall* –'

'Mm,' said Kate. She pressed her forehead to the window and peered down into the street, trying to see if she could spot any of the old gang from the Nunnery. Vanessa's voice raged on in her ear.

'Limp rag, wet fish, flabby, emasculated, hand-knitted *wimp* –'

The bus pulled away. There hadn't been anyone there that Kate knew.

'– *scream* if he doesn't!'

'Doesn't what?' said Kate.

'*Give* something!' snarled Vanessa. 'You have no idea what it's like having to act with a *eunuch*.'

Kate sunk her chin into the neck of her sweater. She wished Vanessa wouldn't shout words like eunuch in public places. Half the bus must be looking at them.

'So what would *you* call it?'

Kate wouldn't call it anything.

'I think he's just having problems with this one particular part.'

'So what about the way he behaves in PD? *And* that night you went to the cinema with him!'

Kate felt her hackles rise. 'What's that got to do with it?'

'Like a wet fish on a slab!'

'Just because –' Kate dropped her voice a decibel or so – 'just because he didn't slobber all over me doesn't mean he's what you said!'

'I said he was a wimp!'

'You said he was –'

'I meant *emotionally*.'

He hadn't even held her hand in the cinema. But that didn't prove anything. It could simply be – one had to face the truth about oneself – that Ned didn't go for short-haired, flat-chested, snub-nosed dwarves. It could be that she had nothing to offer him; that he preferred mature, sophisticated types with shoulder-length hair and legs up to their ears.

Types like Vanessa.

Except that Ned and Vanessa couldn't stand each other.

'Anyway,' she said, remembering that in spite of her seeming sophistication Vanessa didn't actually know any more about men than she did, 'they don't all behave like raving sex maniacs the first time they take a person out . . . some of them respect a person's feelings.'

Vanessa gave a short laugh. 'Can you see Danny?'

'Oh, well! Danny.'

'Danny has balls,' said Vanessa. (Kate cringed again, into the neck of her sweater.) 'Danny isn't scared of showing emotion. *He* doesn't just stand there like a plank of wood. He gives. Ned doesn't give a damn thing. He doesn't even try. He doesn't –'

They were off again. Kate knew from experience that it wasn't an atom of use attempting to change the subject. With Vanessa, you could only weather the storm. This would go on from now until they reached college. It would pick up again tonight and continue in full flood all day tomorrow and very likely the day after. It would be even worse tomorrow, because by then they would have performed their scenes from *Streetcar*, and if Ned turned out to be as dire in performance as he had so far been in rehearsal then Vanessa's rage was going to be fearsome to behold. And tonight they were supposed to be going to a party!

Kate sighed, resting her cheek against the rattling window frame. Some half-term this was going to be . . .

Duologues were due to start at eleven o'clock in the college theatre. Ten-thirty found Kate critically studying her reflection in one of the mirrors in the girls' cloakroom. Did blue-frosted eye shadow and brandy-snap blusher really make her any more Blanche-du-Bois-like, or did it simply make her look like a street-walker? Deciding that it made her look like a street-walker, she sighed and wiped it off again.

Christine, meanwhile, a figure of perfect repose, lay spread out along one of the benches, relaxing. Sara had locked herself in a lavatory, declaring she felt sick, Vanessa had disappeared entirely – which was a nusiance, because Kate had been going to ask her advice as to whether she thought it would be a good idea to stuff some rolled-up tights down her bra. She did so anyway, and stood back to survey the effect.

'What do you think?' She gazed down anxiously at Christine. 'Does it look natural?'

'What?'

'My bosom.'

'You haven't got a bosom.' Christine spoke without opening her eyes.

'I have now,' said Kate. 'Look!'

A flicker of irritation crossed Christine's face. 'I do wish people wouldn't talk at me when I'm trying to prepare.'

'Sorry, I'm sure,' said Kate. Some people! There was a knock at the door, and she went to open it. It was Danny. He goggled when he saw Kate's newly acquired attributes.

'Where did that lot come from?'

'What do you mean, where did it come from? Where do such things usually come from? They grow.'

'Overnight? What you got in there?'

'Never you mind what I've got in there! It's nothing to do with you. You just keep your hands to your – hey!' shrieked Kate. 'Give me back my boob!'

Miss Truscott, who happened to be passing, turned and raised an eyebrow. 'Really!' she said, and stalked on.

'Now you've done it.' Kate snatched at her rolled-up tights. 'I bet they never behaved like that at RADA . . . Look, give it back, you pig! I'm lopsided.'

'I like you better when you're flat,' said Danny. 'I don't go for big-titted women.'

'No, well –' Kate rammed the tights back down her bra. 'I'm not doing it for you, am I? Talk about inflated male egos!'

'It's the female's job,' said Danny, 'to please the male of the species.'

'Crap!' said Kate, borrowing from Vanessa. (She dreaded to think what her mother would say if she could hear some of the language she was using these days.) 'What do you want, anyway? Christine's relaxing.'

'*Preparing,*' said Christine.

'Preparing,' said Kate.

'That's all right,' said Danny. 'I don't want Pristine.' (Pristine Christine was what Ned called her; Danny usually shortened it to Pris.) 'I came to see if Vanessa's here.'

'I don't know where Vanessa is. Did you want her for something?'

Danny said not really; what he really wanted was Ned. He had thought he might be with Vanessa. 'I want to bum a couple of quid off him.'

'I can let you have a couple of quid – well, I can let you have *one*.'

'It's only till tomorrow,' said Danny. 'I got my Saturday job, then.'

'Wait and I'll see what I've got.'

To reach her purse, which was in her locker, Kate had to climb over Christine (who made angry noises of protest). Having got her purse and taken it across to the door, she belatedly remembered that she didn't have anything in it. She had removed all the money at the bus stop that morning and given it to Vanessa for safe keeping.

'The catch has gone –' She demonstrated. 'Everything fell out.'

'Yeah – something else is going to fall out if you're not careful!'

Kate snatched hastily at one of her new bosoms. 'For that you don't *deserve* to be lent money. Anyway, Vanessa's got all mine.' She turned, thought better of trampling over Christine a second time, and hustled out through the door, instead, with Danny. 'Let's go and find them.' It was beginning to get on her nerves, shut away in the cloakroom with only Christine for company, and in any case she still wasn't too certain about the efficacy of rolled-up tights. She would like the benefit of Vanessa's expert opinion before parading them on stage. 'They're probably going through their lines somewhere. Have you tried looking round the studios?'

Together, she and Danny tried the studios, the classrooms, the library, the refectory, the students' lounge. All were either in use, with classes taking place, or occupied by crowds of screaming students.

'What about Studio 6?' said Danny.

'We're not allowed in Studio 6.'

Studio 6, tucked away beneath the main stairs, was strictly out of bounds. The ceiling was propped up with steel joists, awaiting repair work after Christmas. They couldn't have gone in there. Or could they?

With one eye on the Principal's office, which was rather too close for comfort, they crept along the passage, ducked under the rope barrier, past the sign which said NO STUDENTS BEYOND THIS POINT. As soon as they reached the corner, they heard it – the sound, as Danny said afterwards, of fearsome fishwifing. Vanessa's voice, pitched low and obviously intended as a whisper, nevertheless reached them quite clearly: 'Of all the *gut*less, *spine*-less, *use*less –'

Danny and Kate exchanged glances.

'Novel way to go over lines,' said Danny.

Before Kate could say anything they heard Ned's voice, furious, in reply: 'Listen, loudmouth! Has anyone ever told you what a pain in the fundamental orifice you are?'

Kate suppressed a desire to giggle. No one, to her knowledge, had ever called Vanessa a pain in the fundamental orifice before (though doubtless many had been tempted).

'Sounds like they're having fun,' said Danny.

'Ought we to do something?'

'Do what?'

'Well . . . stop them, or something.'

'What for? They're happy.'

'But they've got to be on stage in ten minutes!'

'So that's their problem.' Danny, losing interest, turned and headed back up the passage. 'Never interfere in domestic squabbles. Only get your nose chewed off.' He stood waiting by the rope barrier. 'You coming?'

Kate hesitated. It didn't seemed right that Vanessa should be allowed to upset Ned only ten minutes before a performance. She obviously *had* upset him. Ned never lost his temper. Trust Vanessa! Old Woodie always did say she was enough to try the patience of a saint.

'Trottie!' Danny jerked his head. 'Stop pratting around!'

Reluctantly she moved away. She still thought it was unfair. Ned had enough problems with the part of Stanley without Vanessa going and adding to them.

'What about the money you wanted?'

'Not the right moment,' said Danny.

'But wha –'

'Look, just leave 'em! It's between the two of 'em, OK?'

She supposed that Danny was right; but *I* would never treat Ned like that, she thought.

Nobody but staff was allowed into the theatre during a performance of duologues. A large notice had been hung on the door saying NO ENTRY: PERFORMANCE IN PROGRESS. Even those who were involved, but who were not yet required on stage, were forbidden as spectators. There was to be, as Mr Morrison put it, 'no wittering in the wings'. Instead, they were to await their turn in the narrow passage which ran alongside the stage, somewhat grandiloquently known as the Green Room. From there they would be summoned by tannoy when it was their turn to make their entrance.

The running order for *Streetcar* was Danny, Christine and Sara, followed by Ned and Vanessa, followed by Kate and Josh. Sara was already there, looking tense, Christine arrived soon after. Josh had yet to put in an appearance.

The tannoy crackled. They heard Mr Morrison's voice: 'Can we have the first lot from Group A, please?'

'That's us,' said Danny. 'Wish us luck!'

Kate held up crossed fingers. She felt lonely after the three of them had gone. She paced a while, muttering her lines and from time to time squinting down at her new bosom to make sure it was still in place. She wished Vanessa would come, so that she could consult her about it. Even now she didn't feel too certain. What if it simply looked like rolled-up tights?

If Ned and Vanessa didn't get a move on they would miss their entrance. The first scene must be almost halfway through by now. She wondered if she ought to risk a last-minute trip back to Studio 6 and alert them? Mr Morrison would be furious if they weren't there when they were called, and he was already quite furious enough with Ned as it was. He had had another go at him the other day, in PD.

'What is it with you? Can't you ever rake up enough energy to get worked up about *any*thing?'

All because Ned hadn't been able to cry on demand. It really wasn't fair! Nobody could cry on demand – well, almost nobody. Sara had been able to, surprisingly enough, and Judy, in Group B, had apparently been in floods. Mr Morrison had told her she was too self-indulgent. That was typical of Mr Morrison. You just couldn't win. If you didn't give him what he wanted, he tore strips off you; and if you did, he still tore strips off you. Which was as nothing to what he was going to do to Ned and Vanessa if they didn't arrive pretty sharpish.

Danny and the other two returned, Sara still looking tense, Christine pink and flustered, Danny enigmatic.

'How did it go?'

Danny lifted his shoulders in an expansive gesture.

'All right,' he said. 'I guess.'

'At any rate, you weren't lynched!'

It had become a joke amongst the four of them, Danny being lynched. 'Daring to lay hands on Our Women,' Ned would say, in his best peppery-colonel voice. 'Gad, sir! Men have been shot for less.' You could make that sort of joke with Danny. There was a black boy in one of the other classes, John Durrant, who would have spat in your face for it. At least, that was the feeling Kate always had. Danny said it was because John Durrant was into black pride. (When Vanessa had asked Danny why *he* wasn't, they had all groaned and Ned had said, 'Do us a favour . . . give it a rest!')

The tannoy began crackling again: 'Can we have the next couple, please?'

Danny and Kate looked at each other.

'Where are they?' said Christine.

Even as she asked the question, the door at the far end of the passage was flung open and Ned and Vanessa stalked through. Their faces were white, their lips tight pursed. They looked like a couple who had just come very close to murdering each other.

'What happened?' said Christine, as in grim-faced silence, looking neither to right nor left, they marched the length of the passage.

'Oh! Who knows?' With the immediate crisis over, Kate was more interested in the effect of her new bosom. 'Look, tell me! Does it look all right? Honestly?'

Christine turned, slowly, to study her. Her mouth dropped open. 'What have you done?'

'I told her,' said Danny. 'Looks daft, doesn't it?'

'I don't think it looks daft,' said Sara. 'I think it looks quite sexy.'

Sexy, huh? Kate swaggered a bit. Christine shook her head.

'It doesn't look like Trottie.'

She didn't want it to look like Trottie, she wanted it to look like Blanche. Sexy, sultry, and southern . . .

'What happens if I poke one?' said Danny. He did so, before she could stop him. 'Cor, look at that! Battered boob!'

'Oh – you!' Kate plunged her hand into her bra and yanked out the tights. She hurled them at him, venomously. 'I just wish they had lead *weights* in them!'

Faintly, from on stage, they heard the sound of voices: urgent and angry. It was exactly the sort of urgency, exactly the sort of anger, that Mr Burge had spent the past six weeks trying in vain to coax out of Ned.

'Sounds almost like the real thing,' said Danny.

There was a moment of silence, then Ned and Vanessa came stalking back into the Green Room. Ned was in the lead, Vanessa following.

'Everything all right?' said Christine, brightly.

'Fine, thank you,' said Vanessa.

Ned didn't say anything; just pushed past Josh,

who was on his way in, and disappeared. Josh turned and looked after him.

'What's his problem?'

'Delayed shock . . . post-natal depression . . . excuse me!'

Vanessa shot out through the door. Danny looked at Kate and pulled a face. The tannoy opened up: 'Can we have the last couple, please?'

'Well, I guess this is it,' said Josh. 'The moment of truth . . .'

A moment, indeed, was all it was. The scene at which they had toiled and moiled for six long weeks was over almost before it had even begun. Kate forgot her private worries about not being sexy enough, not being sultry. For an all too brief space she was Blanche du Bois, cropped hair, freckled face, flat bosom and all.

She couldn't have done it without Josh. Josh was one of the most relaxed people she had ever known, yet at the same time one of the most intense. He moved sparingly, with crouched, almost catlike prowls about the stage, stopping every now and again to pounce, to menace, to demand a reaction. Vanessa, right back as far as the first week of term, had said that of them all, Josh was the one she would most like to direct: the only one of them, she said, who really had what she called personal magnetism. Kate had rather resented it at the time; she began, now, to understand what Vanessa had meant.

Back in the cloakroom Kate looked for Vanessa but didn't find her. What she found instead was Group B frenziedly prinking and preening before the mirrors as they prepared for their own ordeal. She moved through them to get at her locker, only to find Christine once again in possession of the bench.

'Where's Vanessa? Have you seen her?'

Christine shook her head. She was already busy

studying her poem for Voice and Speech that afternoon.

'I think she went off with Ned.'

'Oh.'

Kate hung around the cloakroom for a while, listening to Group B's hysteria and to Christine droning her poem:

April is the cruellest month, breeding
Lilacs out of the dead land, mixing
Memory and desire, stirring
Dull roots with spring rain –

T.S. Eliot; *The Waste Land*. She wondered if Christine really understood it, or if she'd only chosen it to impress. Kate had chosen some Dylan Thomas. It might not be as high-brow as T.S. Eliot, but at least she knew what it was about. (Some of it, anyway.)

Group B, with the martyred air of those about to take their last walk, trooped off to do their duologues. Kate was left alone with Christine, droning her poem. She smothered a yawn.

'Is it lunchtime?'

'What?'

'I said, is it lunchtime?'

'It's twelve o'clock,' said Christine. 'Don't you have a watch?'

She did, but it had fallen between the side of her bed and the wall over a week ago and she hadn't yet bothered to move the bed and dredge it up. Anyway, one oughtn't to need a watch. People were far too time-bound.

'*– Bin gar keine Russin*,' droned Christine. '*Stamm' aus Litanen, echt deutsch –*'

'I think I shall go and look for Vanessa,' said Kate.

On her way down the corridor she bumped into Danny.

'That girl,' he said, 'is a nutter.'

'Vanessa? Why? Where is she?'

Danny said he didn't know where she was *now*, but a few minutes ago she had come waltzing into the boys' cloakroom, cool as you please, demanded to know which was Ned's locker, opened it, taken something out, slammed the locker shut, told Danny that 'I haven't got time to stay and gossip' ('Wonderful manners,' said Kate) and gone swishing off again. Kate rubbed a finger up her nose.

'So where's Ned?'

'*I* dunno.' Danny shrugged. 'Haven't seen him.'

'You don't think she's done him in, do you?'

'Wouldn't put it past her. Wouldn't put anything past her. You coming for lunch?'

Kate hesitated. 'Shouldn't we go and look?'

'What for? I want my lunch!'

'You can have your lunch afterwards.'

'I don't want it afterwards! I want it now.'

Kate looked at him, reproachfully. 'Have you no soul? Ned could be lying somewhere in a pool of blood with that evil woman standing over him and all you can think of is eating!' She grabbed him by the arm. 'Come and help me find them!'

Danny consented, though most unwillingly, to be dragged back down the corridor.

'I don't want to find them. I'm starving. I want my lunch. Why can't we let them get on with it? I don't care what they're up to. My gut's hanging out. I want to eat. I want to –'

'Oh, be quiet!' said Kate. 'We'll just have one quick look in Studio 6. If they're not there –'

'If they're not there, I'm going to have my lunch.'

For the second time that morning Kate and Danny slunk past the Principal's office, for the second time ducked beneath the rope barrier and crept on guilty tiptoe up the passage to the forbidden studio.

'Just get a move on!' said Danny.

'All *right*. Don't be so impatient!' Kate crouched and applied her eye to the keyhole.

You couldn't really see very much through a keyhole. In fact, you couldn't really see anything.

'I want my lunch,' said Danny.

'Quiet!' Kate turned, and pressed her ear to the door crack. 'There's someone in there.'

'Who?'

'I don't know, I can't hear.' She could hear sounds, but they didn't sound like voices.

'Let's have a listen.' Danny elbowed Kate out of the way and pressed his own ear to the crack. He listened for a bit. 'Weird!'

'What do you suppose is happening?'

Danny straightened up. 'Either she's throttling him or –'

'Or what?'

'Or it's blue movie time . . . I'd come away, if I was you.'

'Shouldn't we go in?'

'I wouldn't.'

'Why not?'

Danny looked at her. Kate felt herself blushing.

'*I* don't mind,' she said. To prove it, she rapped smartly on the door. 'Vanessa? Is that you?'

There was a pause, then the door opened and Vanessa appeared.

'What do you want?'

'Is Ned in there?'

'Yes, he is. Why?'

'We just wondered where you were, that's all.'

'So now you know,' said Vanessa. She made as if to close the door.

'But we want some money! For our lunch.

Danny wants to borrow some and I haven't got any. You've got it.'

Vanessa tutted, impatiently. 'Wait there.'

She closed the door in Kate's face. Seconds later it opened again, the merest crack, and Vanessa thrust her purse at Kate. 'Take it.'

'But what ab –'

'Just take it,' said Vanessa, 'and *go*.'

She wasn't left with much in the way of an alternative. She knew better than to argue with Vanessa in one of her moods. Kate walked back, disgruntled, along the corridor with Danny.

'Something funny's going on.'

Danny grunted.

'I'd like to know what!'

'I'd like to have my lunch.'

'You're *going* to have your lunch. You don't think she's done something dreadful, do you?'

'Like what?'

'Like knocked him unconscious or something.'

'Leave it out!' said Danny. 'She's not that butch.'

'She can get very violent when she's in a temper. One time,' said Kate, 'she threw a saucepan at me.' It seemed convenient, for the moment, to forget that that was only after Kate had thrown the washing-up bowl. 'She could have knocked him out and be trying to resuscitate him.'

'Kiss of life, nice!'

'Not if you'd got a fractured skull, it wouldn't be. He could have fallen and hit his head or something . . . she could have *killed* him. You don't think we ought to go back and check? I mean –'

'You can go back,' said Danny. 'I'm going to go and have my lunch.'

He swung up the stairs, towards the refectory.

'Sex and food,' screamed Kate, 'that's all you ever think of!'

'What else is there?' said a voice in her ear.

Kate turned, and saw Gareth Nelson, one of the boys from Group B. She didn't like Gareth Nelson. He fancied himself; really thought he was the big turn-on. He leered at her, suggestively. Great blubber-mouthed creep. Kate turned, and sprang up the stairs after Danny.

'Wait for me, you pig!'

Even if Danny did only think of sex and food, at least she felt safe with him.

6

Neither Ned nor Vanessa put in an appearance during the lunch break. Kate looked for them all over (Danny having long since grown bored and gone off somewhere with Asher) but they were nowhere to be seen. In the end she was forced to give up and sit in the lounge with her Dylan Thomas.

At one-thirty Group A had Voice and Speech with Miss Truscott. To Kate's relief, because by then she had almost begun to persuade herself they had run off together, Ned and Vanessa were both sitting there. So, however, was Miss Truscott, which meant they didn't have a chance to talk. Kate raised both eyebrows as a sign of enquiry, but Ned, very solemn, only winked at her, and Vanessa didn't respond at all. Whether they were back on speaking terms or still in a rage with each other it was impossible to tell. Ned seemed a bit subdued, a bit paler than usual (unless that was just Kate's imagination), but the fact that they had consented to sit on adjacent chairs instead of on opposite sides of the room would appear to indicate that for the moment, at any rate, there had been an outbreak of peace.

One by one, Group A read through the poems they had prepared. Miss Truscott was most enthusiastic about Christine's choice of T.S. Eliot; she didn't seem to care that the woman almost certainly didn't understand a word of what she was reading. When it came to Kate and her Dylan Thomas, Miss Truscott sighed and said: 'Ah, yes! Dear Dylan . . . we can never get away without at least one by him.'

Kate wondered what she meant.

Ned read a First World War poem by Wilfred Owen, *Anthem for Doomed Youth*:

What passing-bells for those who die as cattle?
Only the monstrous anger of the guns.
Only the stuttering rifles' rapid rattle
Can patter out their hasty orisons.

He read it extremely badly, even Kate had to admit it. He mistimed all the breathing, and he quite obviously wasn't keeping his ribs up, which was what they had spent the whole of the first half of term learning to do. Kate held her own breath in painful anticipation as he came to the end, but all Miss Truscott said, with a funny look at Ned, was: 'That's a singularly strange choice for one who intends to make the army his profession – and what, pray, has happened to your breath control? KEEP THOSE RIBS UP!'

He had been let off lightly: Miss Truscott must be in a good mood. Possibly it was the influence of half-term, for even Mr Morrison, in PD, was far from being his normal sadistic self.

'I'm not going to give you full crits on this morning's performances, I'll leave that to Michael. I'll just toss a few observations at you – give you something to think about over the break. Let's see . . . what have we?' He flipped open his notebook, riffling through the pages until he came to the relevant section. 'Here we are! Sara.'

Sara, said Mr Morrison, had to learn how to relax – 'you're just a bundle of nervous tension. Makes me tighten up just looking at you.' Christine had been 'Too superior by half. Too much the Ice

Maiden.' Danny and Kate had both tried hard and 'very nearly pulled it off'. Josh, as expected, was awarded full marks for an excellent performance. Vanessa received praise tempered with caution: 'A trifle over-generous with the emotions. Learn to keep something in reserve. Far more effective used sparingly.'

Ned was left until last. Mr Morrison leafed back a couple of pages in his notes.

'Yes, now! Edward.' There was a moment's awful silence. Kate couldn't bring herself to look at Ned. If he'd been as dire in performance as he had in rehearsal, then this was going to be murder; and after what he'd been through at the hands of Vanessa, she wouldn't have thought he could take very much more. 'What can I say?' It would probably be kinder, thought Kate, if he didn't say anything. 'I was expecting the worst – and I got very nearly the best. I congratulate you!'

Relief flowed in great waves about the room. It came from Kate, from Sara, from Vanessa, from Danny . . . though not, seemingly, from Ned himself. He sat, quite composed, quite calm, as one unmoved by either praise or criticism. But he surely *must* be relieved, thought Kate.

'Of course, it wasn't right,' said Mr Morrison. 'It wasn't Stanley. You couldn't play Stanley in a thousand million years, but that doesn't matter. At least it was honest. For the first time you've shown me that the potential is there. What I want now is to see that potential fulfilled. No more creeping back into that tight little corner. What you've done once, you can do again. After all –' for a moment, Mr Morrison looked almost skittish – 'it wasn't really so very painful, was it?'

Ned pulled a face. 'I guess not.'

'What do you mean, you guess not? You're still

in one piece, aren't you? Haven't fallen off your pedestal? Well, then! From now on, let personal development be your watch-word – and that goes for the rest of you, as well. You'll be doing Shakespeare for your second lot of duologues, but we haven't yet finally decided on the play, so I'm afraid you'll just have to sweat it out until next week. OK!' He picked up his briefcase. 'It's only three o'clock, but you might as well push off, seeing as it's half-term. Enjoy yourselves, don't have too many late nights, don't get drunk, and don't do anything I wouldn't. I want to see you back here, first thing Tuesday morning, fighting fit and rarin' to go – and just be kind to our friend Edward here. Baring his soul has obviously cost him dear!'

Going down to the cloakroom, they bumped into Judy.

'Don't forget,' she said, 'party tonight, my place, nine o'clock. You are all coming, aren't you?'

They confirmed that they were. Even Josh, who tended to be mysterious and do his own thing, was coming to Judy's party.

'See you eight-thirty,' said Danny, as Kate and Vanessa went off for their bus. 'Lewisham Town Hall . . . don't be late!'

Vanessa, on the journey home, carefully didn't mention Ned, or *Streetcar*, or their slanging match of earlier on. Instead, she talked busily of duologues and Shakespeare, of which parts they might be given and in which play – how she wished it could be *Macbeth*, so that she could play Lady Macbeth. Or if not *Macbeth* then *Much Ado About Nothing*, because then she could be Beatrice. Or maybe even *The Merchant*, then Ned could be Bassanio. Bassanio was utterly and absolutely Ned's sort of part. Ned to a tee. And Kate could be Nerissa, and –'

'I nearly died,' said Kate, 'didn't you? When

Morrison said, "*What can I say?*" . . . I really thought he was going to pitch into him again.'

'Yes, well, he didn't,' said Vanessa. 'So that's all right. Of course, if we did *Twelfth Night* he could be Malvolio. And you could be Maria, and –'

'What were you and Ned doing all the time after duologues?'

'Minding our own business. Danny could be Toby Belch. *That* would stretch him.'

'You didn't come into lunch,' said Kate.

'I know, we were talking.'

'For an *hour and a half*?'

A spasm of irritation twitched at the corners of Vanessa's mouth. 'I suppose one is allowed to?'

'What on earth were you talking about?'

'We were having a post-mortem, if you must know.'

'About duologues?'

'Amongst other things.'

Picking over the bones of their quarrel, thought Kate. Except that when she and Danny had listened outside the door there hadn't been any sounds of people talking. It had been more like – well, she didn't know what it had been more like. (Not what Danny had hinted at. That was just Danny. Boys liked to hint at that sort of thing. It seemed to give them a buzz.)

'What was it you went into the boys' cloakroom for?'

'I beg your pardon?'

'What was it you went into the boys' cloakroom for? Danny said you tore in like a maniac and grabbed something and then tore out again.'

'Did he?' said Vanessa. 'Really.'

She plainly had no intention of telling Kate what it was. Kate knew what Danny would say. They had all sat around chanting the word, the four of them, last week in Ned's grandmother's flat in Greenwich, pretending it was one of Miss Truscott's vocal exercises: *con*-dom, *con*-dom, *con*-dom . . . Ned and Danny had found it amusing. So, at the time, had Kate.

'You've gone all red!' said Vanessa. 'That's what comes of being nosy.'

She defended herself, hotly. 'I'm not being nosy! But when people you're supposed to be friends with keep on disappearing all the time and acting all peculiar and being secretive, and anyway you didn't have any *right* to go barging into the boys' cloakroom, there could have been people standing about stark naked for all you knew, you could've embarrassed them, you could've really upset them, I should've thought the *least* you could've done was knock at the door and ask Danny to get whatever it was' (what*ever* it was) 'rather than just go crashing in and being foully rude to people, I mean, I don't call it being nosy just to wonder what's going on when –'

'Oh, shut up, Trottie!' Vanessa turned, moodily, to look out of the window. 'You can't be expected to be let in on *every*thing.'

'I just don't know what the matter is with you two girls . . . forever quarrelling and fighting! What have you got to fight about? We let you leave school, we let you go to college, you're studying what you want to study, what more do you want? And surely to goodness,' said Kate's mother, 'you're not intending to go to a party in *those* clothes?'

Kate and Vanessa looked at each other and rolled their eyes, united, for a moment, in common cause – which Vanessa had to go and ruin the very minute they left the house.

'Honestly,' she said, 'your mother!'

'She can't help it,' said Kate. 'It's the way she was brought up.'

'Yes, and it's the way she's bringing you up, too . . . You want to watch it! You'll be just like her by the time you get to thirty.'

'I will not.'

'Yes, you will, I can see it coming. You're half-way there already. All the nagging and the nitpicking and the nosy-parkering . . . *just* like your mother.'

'I don't nosy-parker! Nor does she.' Kate's mother had about nine million irritating habits, but nosy-parkering was not amongst them. That was being unfair.

'So what do *you* call it?' said Vanessa. 'Always wanting to know where you're going, who you're going with, what time you're going to be back, what –'

'That's not nosy-parkering! Any normal mother would want to know that sort of thing. Of course, you haven't *got* a normal mother. Yours doesn't care tuppence . . . she probably wouldn't care if you were found in a ditch with your throat cut.'

'Don't go bringing my mother into it! She's got nothing to do with it.'

'No, she makes jolly sure of that, doesn't she? Can't say your father has much to do with anything, either. What's he ever contribute?'

'Oh, nothing whatsoever,' said Vanessa, heavily sarcastic. 'He only pays the bills and feeds us all and keeps that nasty little suburban roof over our heads . . . that's all *he* does!'

They quarrelled non-stop all the way to Lewisham. By the time they arrived at their meeting place outside the Town Hall they were both thoroughly disgruntled – and were not made any less so by the discovery that Danny was waiting for them on his own.

'Where's Ned?'

'Ned's in bed.'

'Seriously,' said Kate.

'Seriously,' said Danny. 'Said he might come along later.'

'Why? What's the matter with him?'

'Shock, probably . . . not being yelled at by Morrison.'

'He wasn't just not yelled at,' said Vanessa. 'He was *congratulated*.'

'Yeah. Well – I dunno. Maybe he's a bit of a masochist. Glutton for punishment. Can't get enough of it.'

'Oh, really!' Vanessa, impatient, tossed her head. 'You two carry on. I'll go round and talk some sense into him.'

'Why don't we all go?' said Kate.

'It doesn't need all of us. You two carry on.'

'But s –'

'I'll join you later.'

'But s –'

'Stumm!' Danny took Kate's arm. 'Let's go.'

Reluctantly, Kate allowed herself to be led away. She didn't want to go to the party without Ned. She didn't want Vanessa to go round to the flat by herself. If Ned were in bed, then she wouldn't have thought that he would want it, either. She said so to Danny, but Danny just humped a shoulder.

'She got him into it, she can get him out of it.'

'Out of what?'

'State he's in.'

'What state?'

'Feeling sorry for himself.'

'Why is he f –'

'Look, forget about it,' said Danny. 'We're going to a party, OK? Let's enjoy ourselves.'

The party was quite wild. All of Group B were there, and all of Group A, save for Ned and Vanessa.

There was also a crowd from Judy's old school, plus the people-who-lived-opposite and the people-who-lived-next-door, so that the front room of the Wilsons' rather small terraced house was full to a state of satisfying fug.

'Where are your parents?' yelled Kate, above the pulsating hubbub of music and voices.

'Gone out for the night!'

'*All* night?'

'Until midnight.'

Some parents! Kate was impressed. She wondered if there was any way she and Vanessa could possibly persuade their two to go out for the night and leave her and Vanessa in sole possession. Regretfully, she decided there wasn't.

'Leave you two girls by yourselves? I wouldn't dream of it! I know all about teenage parties, thank you very much . . . get back to find the house a wreckage. People being sick all over the place, drink spilt on the carpet, cigarette burns on the furniture . . . oh, no!'

There were times when Kate could understand why it was that Vanessa grew impatient. Kate often grew impatient herself. In fact, she was growing quite impatient now, only not with her mother. What was Vanessa up to all this time? It was getting on for ten o'clock. If she didn't arrive soon, she might just as well not bother. What were they *doing*, her and Ned?

The more she worried, the more it tormented her. She tried shouting at Danny, 'Do you think they're going to come?' but Danny only hunched a shoulder. He wasn't bothered.

By half-past ten Kate could stand it no longer. There was a telephone in the hall, she had seen it on her way in. She would go out there and ring them; check whether they were still at the flat. She put her mouth close to Danny's ear: 'I'm just going upstairs.' Danny nodded.

'OK.'

She didn't know why she'd told him that. If she *had* been going upstairs she wouldn't have bothered to tell him, she would just have gone. Why couldn't she have said to him, 'I'm going to telephone the flat and see if they're coming?' There wasn't anything to be ashamed of. She wasn't being nosy – she wasn't *spying*. She just wanted to know.

It was natural to want to know. She bet Vanessa would, if it were the other way round.

Fortunately, since she couldn't remember the number, Ned's grandmother's surname was the same as Ned's. There were two and a half columns of Careys in the London telephone book. In furtive haste, fearful even now lest Danny come out and discover her, she ran her finger down them. Carey A, Carey Andrew, Carey A.B., Carey A.C. –

Ned's grandmother came right at the very end: Carey, Winifred. She dialled the number. Vanessa would probably be mad, but she didn't care. She had every *right* to telephone. Ned was her friend just as much as he was Vanessa's. In fact, he was more her friend because he had gone with her to the cinema. He hadn't as yet gone anywhere with Vanessa, and after the way she had bawled at him this morning it would be extremely surprising if he ever did. How appalling for someone who was feeling down to have Vanessa turn up on the doorstep! Vanessa was the very last person you would want. Always so bossy, so know-it-all, so *arrogant*. That was the word for Vanessa: she was *arrogant*. If Kate had gone round there she would have been kind and sympathetic and made cups of tea. She could just see Vanessa marching in, lecturing and haranguing. She bet Vanessa hadn't made a single cup of tea. It wouldn't even occur to her.

Nobody answered the telephone in Ned's grandmother's flat. Kate hung on and hung on but the phone just went on ringing.

In the end, when it became obvious that nobody was there – or that if they were, they had no intention of bestirring themselves – she put the receiver down and went slowly back to the party. A party really wasn't much fun when the person whom you most wanted to be there hadn't come. There was always Danny, of course, and she was grateful for that, because she wouldn't have wanted to be there on her own; but Danny wasn't Ned.

She looked around for Danny and saw that he was in a huddle in the corner with Josh and his guitar. They were probably going to do a number together. In another mood she would have joined them (she had always enjoyed singing; Vanessa was practically tone deaf) but she wasn't feeling very extrovert just at the moment. She felt more like being curled up in bed, in the dark, all by herself with her pain.

Just inside the door, Gareth Nelson was chatting up a giggly thing with spiked hair from Judy's old school. When he saw Kate he winked and said, 'You look as if you need cheering up! Fancy a bit of rough?'

Kate did her best to look straight through him. The giggly thing giggled and said, 'He means rough cider!'

'Here.' Gareth held out a glass. 'Have a taste.'

Warily (because you could never tell with people like Gareth, it could be methylated spirit or something quite disgusting) she took a sip.

'Not bad, eh?' said Giggle. She giggled again. 'You at college with Judy?'

'And me,' said Gareth. 'Don't forget me!'

'I wouldn't do that,' said Giggle.

Kate sipped again at her cider. It wasn't as sweet as the sort she was used to, more like she imagined beer might be, but it was all right. She stood there, drinking cider, watching Josh and Danny without really seeing them, listening to the music without really hearing it, wondering about Ned and Vanessa.

'Want a refill?' said Gareth.

Mechanically, she held out her glass. Giggle said, 'You want to watch that stuff! That's pernicious, that stuff is.'

'It's only *cider,*' said Kate. What did she think? She was twelve years old?

'Weak as witch piss,' said Gareth.

'Witch piss!' said Giggle, all silly and giggly.

Kate took her glass and moved with silent dignity across the room. Josh was playing his guitar, Danny singing. Something about a carnival.

Say goodbye, my own true lover,
As we sing a lovers' song.
How it breaks my heart to leave you,
Now the carnival is gone.
Above, the dawn is waking,
And my tears are falling rain,
For the carnival is over,
We may never meet again.
Like a drum my heart was beating
And your kiss was sweet as wine,
But the joys of love are fleeting
For Pierrot and Columbine.
Now the harbour light is calling.
This will be our last goodbye.
Tho' the carnival is over
I will love you till I die.

It seemed to Kate a terribly sad song. Her own tears started to trickle down her cheeks as she listened. Vanessa always had said she cried too easily.

But she hadn't been able to cry on command, as Sara had. Nor had Vanessa. Vanessa never cried. Where *was* Vanessa? Where was Ned? What were they up to together?

I want him! she thought, and the tears went coursing. I want Ned!

'Eh-up!' said Danny. The song had finished. He had come over and was putting his arms round her. 'What's the problem?'

'Song,' she said.

'What about it?'

'Sad.'

'Sad, yeah. It is sad, isn't it? What you drinking?'

She hiccuped. 'Wish pish.'

'Wish pish?' Danny removed the glass from her and sniffed at it, suspiciously.

' 's only cider,' said Kate. She curled her arms round Danny's neck. 'Baby couldn't ge' drunk'n cider.'

'How much have you had?'

'One glass, two glass –' She hiccuped again. 'You're on!'

'Yeah, and you're drunk!'

'Not drunk.' She tucked her head into his shoulder. '*Hole* me.'

Danny, obligingly, tightened his arms about her. They stood for a few minutes, then: 'You' don' thing,' said Kate, 'they're havin' a fair?'

'Who?'

'Neddanessa.'

'Stuff them,' said Danny. 'How about us?'

'Uzz?' Kate wrinkled her brow. 'Uzz wha'?'

'Having an affair . . . I s'pose you wouldn't, would you?'

'Wouldn' wha'?'

'Have an affair.'

Well, and why not? Why shouldn't she? Ned

didn't want her. She might just as well. What did it matter? *Who cared?*

She tried to tell Danny. She tried to tell him that it was an excellent idea and why didn't they go home and begin straight away; but even as she raised her head to speak, the room upended itself and everything went spinning. Her head dropped back, like a cannon ball, on to his shoulder.

'I knew you was drunk,' said Danny.

The rest of the evening passed in a blur. She had vague memories of Danny holding her head over a sink – of Ned and Vanessa suddenly materializing – of being taken on to a bus and collapsing with her head in Danny's lap – of being deposited with Vanessa at their own front door and Vanessa hissing at her NOT TO MAKE A NOISE.

The last thing she remembered was flopping on to the bed with Jacko on top of her, and Vanessa instructing her that 'If you want to be sick, DO IT IN THE BOWL.'

After that, the night was a merciful blank.

7

Kate spent the whole of Saturday feeling dreadful. Cement-mixers churned in her head, her eyes stared blearily from red-rimmed sockets. Her mother couldn't understand it.

'I hope you haven't been *drinking*,' she said.

'It's the flu,' said Vanessa. 'Everybody at college has got it.'

Vanessa, actually, was quite good about things. She didn't nag, or gloat, or censure. All she said, in the privacy of Kate's bedroom, was, 'Honestly, Trottie, you are such a goon! Fancy drinking rough cider . . . everybody *knows* that stuff is lethal.'

Everybody except Kate. It seemed that everybody knew rather a lot of things that she didn't. She hoisted herself, a trifle querulously, on to one elbow.

'Where did you and Ned get to?'

'Oh, now, don't start on that again! You know where we got to . . . we were round at the flat.'

It was all Vanessa would say. Kate felt too limp and floppy to press her any further, but still she couldn't help wondering. She lay with her face buried in Jacko's ruff, pretending that she was six years old again and that Jacko was a puppy and her father was alive. Everything had been so simple when she was only six years old. No incomprehensible yearnings. No pangs of searing jealousy. WHY WAS VANESSA BEING SO SECRETIVE? People were only secretive when they had something to hide. What did Vanessa have to hide? What was going on between her and Ned?

Ned and Danny weren't at the flat over half-term. Ned had gone down to Devonshire, to spend the time with his mother, the writer of historical biographies (she was currently engaged, he said, doing research on 'some old monk guy who lived in the Dark Ages'), and Danny had gone back to Catford, to be with his family – his father who spilt paint, and his mother who was ace, and the two sisters and one little brother who plagued the life out of him. It seemed it was his little brother's birthday and that Danny had to be there for the party, which made Kate think that the little brother couldn't be nearly as much of a pain as Danny sometimes liked to make out.

'Well, of course he isn't,' said Vanessa. (Vanessa was always so *sure* about everything.) 'That's just Danny, putting it on . . . trying to make out he's not involved. Doesn't fit the old macho image.'

'How do you know it's an image?' demanded Kate. 'It might be for real. You were the one that said –'

'I do wish you wouldn't keep quoting me!' said Vanessa. 'It grows very tiresome if one can't ever say anything without having it thrown up at one . . . Actually, if you want to know, I think Danny probably *is* quite macho. More than Ned. Ned's just stiff upper lip and all collywobbles underneath.'

'Ned's sensitive,' said Kate.

'So what's he doing, joining the army?'

'You can have sensitive soldiers!'

'Don't make me laugh,' said Vanessa.

That night, Kate dreamed about Ned being sensitive. She dreamt that Mr Morrison was shouting at him, 'You're all stiff upper lip and collywobbles underneath!' And in the dream, Ned's stiff upper lip began to unstiffen and to grow soft and bendy, like rubber, and his body began slowly to dissolve, to melt, until nothing was left but a mound of pink jelly on the floor, which Vanessa wiped up with a floor cloth. Vanessa kept saying, 'Soldier! Don't make me laugh!'

On Tuesday morning as they went up the road to the bus stop, Kate said: 'I hope Ned comes back.'

Vanessa turned on her, sharply. 'What do you mean, you hope he comes back? Why shouldn't he come back?'

Kate said, 'Well – Morrison –' But Vanessa tossed her head.

'He'll have to put up with worse than Morrison if he's going into the army. Anyway, Morrison was pleased with him . . . of course he'll come back!'

She seemed very positive. Nonetheless, Kate was relieved, as they walked into the students' lounge, to see Ned's familiar figure, wearing the usual blue jeans and sweater, with green combat jacket, drinking a cup of stewed sick from the stewed-sick machine. (It was Ned himself who had christened it that.) He waved at them across the room.

'Morning, Trottie! And how are we this morning? Walking unaided on our own two feet, I'm glad to note!'

'Having lain prostrate on our back all weekend,' said Vanessa.

Ned affected a double take. 'What, my dear Harridan! Does your tongue yet clack? I'm surprised you haven't caught it in a threshing machine long since!'

Vanessa turned, confidentially, to Kate. 'Such charming manners they teach them at these great schools of ours . . . Where was it you went? Eton, did you say?'

'If you persist in spreading that rumour,' said Ned, 'I shall have you up for slander.'

'Why *won't* you tell us?' said Kate.

'I might . . . one day.' Ned grinned. He seemed to be looking at Vanessa. 'If you choose your moment.'

Just for a second, Kate thought that Vanessa grew pink; but perhaps it was merely a trick of the light. Vanessa wasn't a girl for blushing. In any case, what was there to blush about?

In Duologues, later in the day, they learnt which play they were to do for the second half of term. Mr Burge had pinned a sheet of paper on the door. It said:

DUOLOGUES – GROUP A – OTHELLO

Act IV, Sc. 2

Othello . . . . Ned Carey
Emilia . . . . Vanessa Bland
Desdemona . . . . Kate Cochrane
Iago . . . . Danny McEvoy
Rodrigo . . . . Joshua Levy

Act IV, Sc. 3

Desdemona . . . . Sara Miller
Emilia . . . . Vanessa Bland

Act V, Sc. 2

Othello . . . . Joshua Levy
Desdemona . . . . Christine Cooper

Mr Burge explained that it was not he but Mr Morrison who had been responsible for the casting.

'So if you're wondering why it is that honey over there' (he jerked a thumb at Vanessa) 'isn't playing Desdemona, and why matey here' (with a nod at

Danny) 'isn't playing Othello, you'll know where to go for the answers. Doubtless he has his reasons; he usually does. In the meantime, let us read through and acquaint ourselves with the text.'

In the students' lounge, later, there was the usual shrill babble from those who considered themselves to have been badly treated. Group B were there, milling about like headless chickens in a hen coop, all of a huff and a fluster because they'd been assigned *A Midsummer Night's Dream,* and Gareth Nelson was to be King of the Fairies and Judy was to be Titania, and what they wanted to know was, WHO DID MORRISON THINK HE WAS KIDDING? It was becoming increasingly obvious, said Judy, that the man was a psychopath.

'Just trying to humiliate us . . . trying to make us look ridiculous!'

'You think *you're* going to look ridiculous?' Ned gave a short laugh. 'How do you think I'm going to look? Trying to play Othello, with *this* –' he punched Danny on the arm – 'playing Iago?'

'And would you believe,' wailed Vanessa, 'that I've got to play Emilia when I have always, *always* as long as I can remember, wanted to play Desdemona?'

'And wouldn't I be lovely as Iago?' said Ned.

'White trash, him bellyache,' said Danny. 'Go get yourself a tin of boot polish!'

'Yes, and you know what he'd say then?' Ned took up his mad-Morrison stance, eyes glaring, features contorted. 'WHAT THE DEVIL ARE YOU HIDING YOURSELF FOR? WHAT'S THE MATTER WITH YOU? YOU SOME KIND OF A RECLUSE?'

'We have to remember,' said Christine, 'that it is being done for a purpose.'

'Yeah, yeah, yeah, we've got to stretch ourselves . . . don't tell me, I know! It's all a bit too obvious.'

It might have been obvious in Ned's case –

Othello's jealousy over Desdemona was a direct parallel with that early exercise in PD, when he'd refused to fight Danny over the girl-who-had-gone-out-with-both-of-them – but Kate really couldn't see any special reason for her having been given the part of Desdemona. She was very glad that she *had* been given it (since it meant she was playing opposite Ned), but it didn't seem to her to have any relevance to anything that had gone before, or to any particular problems that she might have.

She discovered that afternoon, in PD, what the relevance was. There was an exercise much beloved of Mr Morrison, known by Group A as 'the dreaded letter scene', which he sprang upon them at intervals without any warning. 'Right! You! You've just received a letter containing bad news. Convey it to me.'

The first person he had sprung it on had been Danny, who had speedily reduced them all to tears. The only problem was, the tears had been tears of laughter. Mr Morrison had not been pleased. He had accused Danny of playing the buffoon: of having embarrassed himself with a display of emotion then resorted to cheap tricks to cover it.

'Anything to save face . . . in other words, *dishonest*!'

Everyone, by now, had been sprung upon except Kate and Ned. Kate had known the axe would have to fall sooner or later. Today was the day when it did so.

'You!' Mr Morrison pointed. 'Letter scene! Right?'

Danny caught her eye and pulled a commiserating face; Ned gave her the thumbs-up. Kate, resigned, walked out to the front. To tell the truth, she wasn't as apprehensive as she might have been. She had made up her mind weeks ago what her letter was going to be about. It wasn't going to be about her mother writing to her when she was away from home to say that Jacko had got run over, which was the first (and most ghastly) piece of bad news which had occurred to her. She knew if she talked about Jacko she would start crying, and nobody wanted to do that; not in front of people. So what it was going to be was a letter from Mr Morrison telling her that he thought her performance in *Streetcar* was the worst thing he had ever seen and that she would never make an actress in a thousand million years, so why not just forget about it and switch courses? 'Go and learn cookery or something'.

Privately Kate was of the opinion that it was rather smart of her to have chosen such a theme. Mr Morrison, perversely, seemed unimpressed. All he said when she had finished was, 'All right. Now move your chair to the far side of the room – go on! As far as you can. I want a good lot of space between you and the rest of us . . . right! It's the end of the day. Everyone's gone home and locked you in. Done it quite deliberately. Gone off and left you. Yes?'

Kate swallowed and said, 'Y-yes.' It was slowly becoming clear to her that something, somewhere, had gone wrong. Mr Morrison never passed over a scene without comment unless he had a reason. She shivered slightly . . . this was the time to start worrying.

'Right. Now – plead with them. You can see them outside, getting ready to go. It's up to you whether they let you out or not. You others –' he gestured – 'turn you chairs round so that you've got your backs to her. If she really makes an impression on you, you can turn round again. But not unless. OK.' He nodded at Kate. 'Plead!'

She pleaded and pleaded, but nobody turned round.

'Look, come on!' she cried. 'Don't be rotten! Stop messing about!'

'They're not messing about,' said Mr Morrison. 'They've done it on purpose because they don't like you. It's up to you to make them change their minds.'

'Look, *please*!' shouted Kate. 'This is stupid – this is *childish*! I've got to get home!'

'You'll have to do better than that,' said Mr Morrison. 'That won't make them change their minds.'

Kate began to grow angry. 'Well, what do you want? What's the point of it?'

'Try making them feel sorry for you . . . move them! Plead with them! Go down on your knees and beg!'

Beg? From that lot? Kate's chin went up. She was damned if she would! There was such a thing as pride. She was starting to hate them, sitting there with their backs turned.

'Danny!' she yelled. 'Let me out!'

Danny sat there, unmoved.

'Vanessa – Ned!' Surely Ned would help her?

She waited until it became obvious that he wasn't going to.

'Christine?' Not much use appealing to her. 'Sara?' Her voice wavered. 'Josh?'

'Oh, the hell with it!' Josh turned, slowly, on his chair. Of them all, he was the most unpredictable. 'Let her out, I can't stand the racket.'

The relief that flooded over her was as great as if she really had been shut in and left. She made to get up, but Mr Morrison waved her back.

'Oh, no, you don't! I haven't finished with you. All right, you others, you can turn yourselves round.' They did so, sheepishly, not meeting Kate's eye. 'Well?' said Mr Morrison. 'Was nobody moved?'

Silence.

'Was nobody made to feel mean or rotten?'

More silence. Then: 'Maybe, like, on a personal level,' said Danny.

'You mean that as her friend you felt you ought to help her out, but as a fellow student, in all conscience, you couldn't.'

'Yeah.' Danny looked across at Kate. 'Something like that.'

'And the reason you couldn't is plainly and simply that her appeal fell flat. Anyone care to say why it fell flat?'

'She didn't humble herself,' said Christine.

The nerve of the woman! Why should she?

'She didn't make us feel that we'd hurt her,' said Vanessa. 'Only that she was mad at us. If we'd thought we were hurting her, we'd have let her out.'

'Precisely.' Mr Morrison turned his attention back to Kate. 'You know what your trouble is, don't you?' he said. 'You're scared of making a spectacle of yourself.'

'No, I'm not,' said Kate.

The words came out before she could stop them. But really, the unfairness of it all! Had she not, in her last term at the Nunnery, for the end-of-term play, taken the part of a comic charlady and made herself up to look all fat and fifty-ish, with a scarf tied round her head and cushions stuffed down the front of her apron? No one who could go on stage looking like that could be accused of being scared to make an spectacle of herself. People had fallen about just at the sight of her.

She said as much, self-righteously, to Mr Morrison. Mr Morrison made a noise of contempt.

'Dressing up! Anyone can make a idiot of themselves dressing up. You're camouflaged, aren't you? Got things to hide behind . . . funny clothes, funny make-up' (Ned pulled a face), 'funny voice. But what about when you're naked and unprotected? That's what I'm interested in. You get out there on your own and you'll find you can't do it. Can't get down on your knees and say, *please don't do this to me . . .* that's what I want from you. If you're scared, show you're scared; if you're hurt, show you're hurt. Do you understand what I'm talking about? Or do you think I'm being unfair?'

Kate thought about it. Reluctantly, she grinned. She felt the dimples coming into her cheeks, and stuck her two index fingers into them to fill the holes. Stupid things, dimples. Little-girlish and *stupid*.

'I did think you were being unfair . . . but now I don't think I do.'

'I want you to be certain.'

'All right,' said Kate. 'I'm certain.'

'Good. So have a close look at the scene you're doing in *Othello*, and understand why it is that you're doing it . . . I shall expect results!'

Desdemona *Upon my knees, what doth your speech import?*
I understand a fury in your words,
But not the words.

Othello *Why, what art thou?*

Desdemona *Your wife, my lord; your true and loyal wife.*

Othello *Come, swear it, damn thyself;*
Lest, being like one of heaven, the devils themselves
Should fear to seize thee: therefore be double-damned. Swear thou art honest.

Desdemona *Heaven doth truly know it.*

Othello *Heaven truly knows that thou art false as hell.*

Desdemona *To whom, my lord? With whom? How am I false?*

Othello *Ah, Des –*

'OK, hang on! Let's hold it there a minute. Trottie, honey –' even Mr Burge had now decided that her name was Trottie – 'you're still not hitting quite the right note. I know the guy's accusing you of being a whore and sleeping around, and you probably feel like kicking his teeth in for him, but that's Trottie; it's not Desdemona. Remember, she loves this man – and when she says 'my lord', she means just that. This is pre-women's lib; none of your rubbishing modern notions about equality, due apologies to Vanessa over there. Desdemona knows her place. She doesn't crawl, she doesn't lose her dignity – but neither does she wade into the attack. I want more the quality of . . . pleading. *To whom, my lord? With whom? How am I false?* She's begging him – tell me! How have I offended you? *Alas, what ignorant sin have I committed?* Do you see what I'm getting at?'

'Yes.' It was what Mr Morrison had been trying to tell her. *If you're scared, show you're scared: if you're hurt, show you're hurt*. Desdemona was scared by Othello's fury, just as she was hurt by his false accusations.

'OK?' said Mr Burge. 'Fine. And Ned, my son –' He laid a hand on Ned's shoulder. 'If you could give it a bit more stick? A bit less of the sophisticated city gent and a bit more of the old jungle drums? This man's a soldier, remember.' ('Ha!' from Vanessa.) 'He's a man of action, not an intellectual. He follows his instincts. Whatever you do, you don't want to over-civilize him. All right! Let's try taking it again from the top.'

Twice more they ran the scene, but it had to be said: Othello really wasn't Ned's part any more than Stanley had been. When Josh played Othello, in the death scene, he was like some magnificent wild beast, all power and unleashed fury. Ned, by contrast, was stiff and self-contained. The nearest he could come to fury was a kind of cool sarcasm. Kate thought it was mean of Mr Morrison to have given him two such unsuitable parts one after the other. It didn't seem to her that it was fair. It wasn't fair to Ned, it wasn't fair to the person playing opposite him.

Rather shyly (because she still wasn't as much at her ease with Ned as she was with Danny) she asked him after class whether he thought it would be a good idea for them to get together, just the two of them, for an extra rehearsal.

'Sure,' said Ned. 'When do you want to do it? Tonight?'

'Tonight would be fine,' said Kate.

When she told Vanessa, Vanessa said, 'Oh, right. OK! You'd better call home and say we'll be late.'

Kate stared, her cheeks turning slowly crimson. Vanessa surely didn't think that *she* was coming?

'It's just the two of us,' she said. 'For our scene.'

'Well, but it's my scene too,' said Vanessa.

'Only bits of it. The bit we're going to work on is the bit between me and Ned.'

'So you'll need someone there to direct you – give you your notes. It'll be good practice for me.'

Kate's bosom (what there was of it) swelled indignantly. Vanessa had absolutely no right to come barging in! She hadn't been invited – and she most certainly wasn't wanted. She was still trying to think of a way of telling her when Ned and Danny arrived.

'Ready?' said Ned. He seemed, automatically, to include Vanessa, just as Vanessa, automatically, had included herself. 'Pop upstairs for a quick bite before we go?'

'Good idea,' said Vanessa. 'Trottie, are you going to call home? You know what your mother's like. Five minutes late –' she set off, along the corridor, with Ned – 'and she's on the phone to the police telling them we've been abducted.'

Kate, left behind with Danny, could only console herself with the reflection that it was still her and Ned who were going to be doing the rehearsal, not Vanessa. Vanessa, actually, had nothing to do with it.

The trouble with Vanessa – *one* of the troubles with Vanessa – was that she simply wasn't capable of being anywhere *without* having something to do with it. First of all she said that she would be on the book so that she could prompt them when they dried. Then she started directing them, trying to alter their moves and suggesting different inflections, even daring to offer her own personal criticisms.

'Trottie, don't *gabble*. Take your time . . . Ned, you're playing Othello as if he's captain of the cricket eleven. Could we have a bit less of the jolly decent chap and a bit more of the old black ram?'

Danny, stretched out on the sofa bed which he used for sleeping on at night, gave a coarse guffaw.

'It's what it says,' said Vanessa. '*An old black ram is tupping your white ewe*.'

'Nice,' said Danny.

Kate blushed. Ned said. 'There's an awful lot of smut in Shakespeare. Have you noticed? They obviously had very smutty minds.'

'*Look*,' said Vanessa, 'this man is a *soldier*.'

'So?'

'So it's what Mr Burge was saying . . . he's a man of action, not an intellectual. *You* ought to know,' said Vanessa, 'about soldiers.'

'Nasty rough things,' said Danny.

'Mindless political automata!' snapped Vanessa.

'That just shows how little *you* know.' Ned sat himself down, back to front astride a chair. 'Contrary to what you obviously imagine, the modern army does not consist of nothing but brain-damaged oicks.'

'No – they never had any brains to get damaged in the first place!'

'Cheap,' said Ned. 'Very cheap.'

'Well, all right!' Vanessa was usually pretty fair in argument; one had to give her that. But why did she always, *always*, have to start one? Kate opened her mouth to intervene, but Vanessa already had the bit well between her teeth. 'So maybe some of them do have brains, it's just that they're not allowed to use them. Because let's face it, all they are is pawns . . . government pawns! Go where they're sent, do what they're told, ours not to reason why . . . What's changed since the days of the Light Brigade? *What's changed?*'

'I'll tell you what's changed! What's changed is that the modern soldier *thinks*.'

'And what good does that do? If you're told to go somewhere and shoot at people, what good's *thinking*? You still have to go there and shoot, don't you? If you'd been in the army a few years ago, I suppose you'd have gone bleating off to the Falklands along with the rest of the sheep?'

Kate groaned. The Falklands was one of Vanessa's favourite hobby horses . . . the Falklands, Northern Ireland, apartheid, Palestinian refugees . . . Kate's mother had had to ask her 'not to talk about these things any more. I'm scared your father will have a fit'.

'Fight for Queen and country, defend our way of life . . . the *hypocrisy*! And people *swallow* it!'

Watching Ned, Kate could see him stiffen slightly.

'It may come as news to you,' he said, 'but not everyone happens to share your particular point of view. There are those who might even call it perverse.'

'Yes, and there are those who might call yours reactionary! Not to mention downright Fascist!'

'Oh, don't be so fatuous!' said Ned.

'All right, so tell me, with all this *thinking* you're supposed to do . . . what do *you* think it is? If it isn't jingoism? Get people going, wind them up, whip them into a frenzy . . . anything, so they'll go out there and do their master's bidding. Go out and conquer, go out and kill –'

'Go out and be killed!'

'Yes! Dead right! Go out and *be* killed. And then everybody rationalizes and says oh, but it was for democracy, for freedom, for *our way of life*, and that makes it all glorious and radiant and wonderful instead of just mean and pointless and squalid . . . like that poem you read for Aggie. That showed you how squalid it was. How disgusting. How *shameful*.'

'For crying out loud! That was the First World War!'

'So what's changed?' screeched Vanessa. She always became so dreadfully angry. Ned, too, was beginning to lose his cool. Kate could see him fighting, almost physically, to remain calm. 'People slaughtering each other in droves just because they're told to. Because that's what you're there for . . . to do what they tell you, no matter what! From the time you join that mob to the time you leave, you're going to have to carry out orders whether you agree with them or whether you don't, even if you think they're morally wrong – even if you think they're criminal. Even if they might give you *nightmares*. How can you possibly justify that?'

'Don't,' said Danny. He positioned himself, fairly and squarely, between Ned and Vanessa. 'Just don't. Just leave it.' He looked hard at Ned. 'Yes?'

Ned took a breath. Vanessa said, 'You shut up, Danny McEvoy! What's it to you? You're not the one who's selling out!'

'No, I'm just the one who has to live here with him!'

'So what?'

'So I'm telling you . . . give it a rest!'

Vanessa threw back her hair. 'He'll have to learn

how to fight his own battles,' she said.

'I can fight my battles, thank you! When the time is right. I thought we were supposed to be having a rehearsal? Poor old Trottie –'

Vanessa made a noise of disgust. Poor old Trottie, sitting on the hearth rug, looked up at the clock and thought, we'll have to be leaving in ten minutes . . .

They'd had almost no rehearsal at all. She knew Vanessa ought never to have come.

8

There were some people, thought Kate, who were definitely born lucky. Vanessa was one of them. One morning in Duologues they were told that Christine had broken her ankle, as a result of which she wouldn't be able to act for the rest of term. It was Vanessa who was chosen to take over from her in the death scene. Not Sara, not Kate; but Vanessa.

Kate couldn't help wondering whether Mr Burge (or would it be Mr Morrison?) had a thing about her. Some men *did* go silly over young girls, and if anyone was going to be gone silly over it would be Vanessa.

Christine came back a few days later, limping, with her right foot in plaster, surrounded by an air of self-important martyrdom. She had fallen off a kerb, she said, in Bromley High Street: an immense fat woman with a shopping trolley had pushed her.

'I might have been *killed*.' Tenderly, as if it were a piece of precious porcelain, she placed her injured foot on a chair. Already people with no taste for originality had scrawled their names on her plaster cast. 'I suppose it's made Vanessa happy?'

'Yes,' said Kate. Vanessa was ecstatic. She kept going round telling people how she had always, *always* wanted to play Desdemona.

'I don't care,' said Christine. 'She's welcome. I wasn't looking forward to it anyway. Not with Josh. Every time we used to get to that bit where he has to put a pillow over my face, I used to think my last hour had come . . . I mean, *really*. Not just acting. If you ask me, he's downright dangerous.'

'Vanessa doesn't seem to mind.' Vanessa still maintained that Josh had more talent than any of them.

'Oh, well! Vanessa. She's so thick-skinned she probably doesn't even notice.' Christine shifted her foot slightly, so that Kate could see, scrawled across the top of the cast, the name Paul Morrison. 'I shouldn't be surprised if he's on drugs.'

'*Josh*?' (Imagine Mr Morrison sinking to that level. That meant he probably had gone silly.)

'The way he carries on.' Christine said it grumblingly, almost censoriously. She sounded, for a moment, like Kate's mother. 'I mean, the way he *dresses* – and I'm sure he doesn't wash.'

'He lives in a squat,' said Kate.

'That's no excuse for not washing, and anyway, *why* does he live in a squat? He's got a home to go to.'

'Maybe he was turned out.'

'Yes, I'd jolly well turn him out,' said Christine, 'going around like some tramp.'

You could tell exactly, thought Kate, how Christine was going to end up in a few years: a middle-aged bigot, married, with two children (nicely spaced out) living in a semi-detached in Bromley. The sort of woman who dusted underneath the ornaments rather than going round. The sort of woman who *had* ornaments. (The sort of woman who dusted.) She was worse than Vanessa. Vanessa might be self-opinionated, but at least she wasn't small-minded. So what if Josh *was* a bit scruffy and had holes in his shoes and didn't always shave? Kate would have given anything to do the death scene with him.

She had come to the conclusion, very reluctantly,

that Desdemona wasn't her role; Emilia was what she ought to have been playing. (Always the serving wench, never the star. You're too *short* to be a star.) She was still convinced that she *could* play Desdemona if only she had a really strong Othello. Nobody could have called Ned a strong Othello. Had it been he who was in the death scene instead of Josh, Christine need never have feared that her last hour had come. Ned's Othello would suffocate his Desdemona with about as much passion as a Noël Coward hero lighting a cigarette. Josh, on the other hand, did it with a kind of agonized savagery that had people on the edge of their seats even when they were seeing it for the fifth or sixth time. Nobody could fail to be a success as Desdemona with Josh for their Othello. It was so unfair!

What made it worse was that it was Ned she was acting opposite. She had so much wanted to act with Ned. She had imagined all the private rehearsals they would have – how Ned (in the character of Othello) would seize her by the wrists and drag her towards him; how his passion would get the better of him and (in the character of Ned) he would pull her into his arms and smother her with kisses . . . Sadly she had to admit that Ned didn't seem to have any passion; not, at any rate, where she was concerned. Four weeks into rehearsal and his rendering of Othello was no different now from how it had been on the very first day: beautifully spoken and emotionally dead.

She grouched about it coming in on the bus one morning with Vanessa, thinking that for once they would find common ground, but to her indignation Vanessa's only response was a tart, 'You know what they say . . . a bad workman always blames his tools.'

The cheek of it! When she had spent practically the whole of the first part of term *whingeing*.

Vanessa, when this was pointed out to her, said loftily that she was not in the habit of whingeing. She may have got a bit heated – a *bit*! – but she had never tried claiming it would be Ned's fault if she turned in a poor performance.

There was an element of truth in this: Vanessa rarely did blame other people for her own shortcomings.

'Well, all right.' Kate struggled for a moment with her pride. 'Maybe I'm just not very good as Desdemona.'

'It's not your part.'

'No, it's not!' She seized on it, eagerly. 'I ought to be Emilia, but he's gone and made me do Desdemona, and I'm supposed to be being vulnerable and scared and how can I be vulnerable and scared if there's nothing to be vulnerable and scared *about*?'

Vanessa, vaguely, as if it weren't a subject that held all that much interest for her, said: 'Maybe he'll come to it like he did for *Streetcar*.'

'That was only because you bawled him out.' Kate remembered Vanessa, in Studio 6, yelling like a fishwife. She knew she couldn't bring herself to do that; not to Ned. Apart from anything else, she still felt too shy with him. She became aware that Vanessa was looking at her, oddly.

'How do you know I bawled him out? Did he tell you?'

'N-no. No! I just – assumed. I mean –' *I just happened to be bending down with my ear to the keyhole* . . . 'I mean, you're always bawling him out.'

'That's because he's such an idiot,' said Vanessa. 'Going into the army!'

'Some people might say you were an idiot,' retorted Kate, 'going into the theatre.'

'At least I'm not going into it to kill people.'

'Ned's not going into the army to kill people, he's

going into it to defend them.' To defend people like Vanessa, as a matter of fact.

'Don't give me that!' said Vanessa. 'That's all claptrap and you know it.'

'Well, anyway –' Kate said it hastily, before Vanessa could embark on one of her diatribes – 'I really don't see what it's got to do with you. It's Ned's life, not yours. Why can't you just leave him alone? All you ever do is nag at him.'

'Someone's got to.'

'Why?'

'Because it's such a stupid waste, that's why! And if nagging's the only way to stop him, then I shall jolly well nag!'

Kate tossed her head. (It wasn't as effective as when Vanessa did it: she didn't have the hair.) 'I'm not surprised he calls you the Harridan!'

She had the satisfaction of seeing Vanessa blush slightly, though being Vanessa she stood her ground.

'I don't care what he calls me. He can call me whatever he likes. All I'm doing is just trying to get him to *think*.'

All she was doing was just irritating him and ruining other people's scenes that they had to act with him. But it wasn't the least bit of use arguing with her. You never *could* win an argument with Vanessa.

Later that day, they had Duologues. There was only time for Ned and Kate to run their scene once: it was as bad as ever it had been. Most of the class was taken up with Josh and Vanessa playing their death scene. Everyone seemed to think it only fair, given that Vanessa had taken over the part at the last minute. Kate supposed that it was (if you considered it fair that Vanessa should have been given the part in the first place) but that did nothing to solve her own problems. Time was running out: there was less than a fortnight to go before performance and she knew she was still playing Desdemona like some kind of stuffed doll.

She had to have more rehearsal. She decided that she would be brave and tell Ned so – and this time she would insist that it was just the two of them. No Danny, no Vanessa; just her and Ned. She didn't care if he did think she was trying to get off with him. Not that it would be anything to be ashamed of even if she were; but anyway, she wasn't. She simply wanted to get things right.

In English, which followed Duologues, they were given back some poems which they had been set to write earlier in the term. The subject proposed had been 'Things that you think about'. Kate had written a poem about Jacko. It began, 'I'm an old dog now, and my day is nearly done' and ended, 'The sands of time are slipping fast, the race is almost run.'

She had cried as she wrote it. She had written poetry before, at the Nunnery, but she had never written anything which had made her cry.

She hadn't let Vanessa read it because Vanessa tended to be snooty about Kate's poetry. Facile was the way she described it. Vanessa had let Kate read hers. It was called 'Mutation' and was all about life after a nuclear holocaust. Kate thought it quite horrid.

At the foot of Kate's poem when it was returned to her Mrs Lockhart, their English tutor, had written her comments: 'Somewhat derivative, I feel. A touch old-fashioned?' It just confirmed Kate in her belief that poetry really was not her scene.

'Mutation' was read out to the class. So was Ned's offering. Ned's didn't have a title. It went on for two pages and was very strange. Kate didn't understand a word of it. She strongly suspected that Ned didn't, either, because when Mrs Lockhart asked if he could explain it to them he said that he couldn't. (Or wouldn't, or didn't want to.) Vanessa took it upon herself to state categorically that it was about life after the bomb. Christine suggested it was a fear of insanity. Sara thought it was like a painting by Salvador Dali, somebody else said Hieronymus Bosch. Kate said she thought it was probably the result of a bad dream.

'Nightmare after Eating Cheese Late at Night,' said Danny.

Kate asked him later if *he* had understood it.

'Me?' said Danny. 'Just down out my tree? Understanding big words like that?'

'No, seriously! Did you?'

'I'll tell you something,' said Danny. 'I don't reckon poetry's written to be understood. Not these days. If you can understand it, then it's no good.'

'So what did you write?' said Kate.

Danny held out his folder. Kate read:

Imagine
If you turned white overnight
All them blacks out there taking your jobs and being out-of-work scroungers and living on the dole at the same time
As well as mugging all your old folk and raping all your women and causing nasty rough riots on all your lovely housing estates
Not to mention bringing horrible AIDS into the country
Wot a fright!

Underneath, Mrs Lockhart had written, 'Interesting'.

'But she didn't read it out,' said Kate.

'Well, she wouldn't, would she?' Danny sounded quite cheerful about it. 'Too easy to understand, in't it?'

'I suppose so.'

Kate fell silent. She was thinking how little one really knew anybody. Ned writing long mad poems that made no sense, Danny writing about how it would be to turn white. *Oh, you're just talking about colour! That's not important*. It might be to Danny, Vanessa had said. *'Course it's not! That sort of thing doesn't bother him*. Not Danny, he was far too happy-go-lucky.

Or was he?

She looked at him, frowning.

'You coming for lunch?' said Danny.

Ned and Vanessa were in the refectory. They were sitting together at a table by the windows, going through Ned's poem line by line.

' ". . . the torrent comes" – *what* torrent?

' "Darkness prevails" – *what* darkness?

' "Faceless beings wander in torment" –' Vanessa jabbed with her finger, accusingly. 'What else *can* it mean?'

'That's assuming, of course, that it means anything.'

'Now you're sounding like Kate and Danny!'

'Thanks very much,' said Danny.

'Was that intended as a compliment?' said Kate.

Ned grinned, briefly. Vanessa simply continued as if they weren't there.

'Whether you meant to or not, the fact is you've painted the most extraordinarily vivid picture of what it would be like. So even if it was only subconscious –'

'You gonna eat all them beans?' said Danny, pointing at the vast mound on Kate's plate.

'Don't expect so. Why? D'you want some?'

'Stop you getting fat.'

Kate held her stomach in. She had a dread of getting fat. Her mother was distinctly pudgy.

'. . . just shows,' said Vanessa, 'that deep down it's something that worries you.'

'Well, of course it worries me! It worries everyone. Doesn't it?'

'Talking of being worried,' said Kate, 'I –'

'Everyone of any normal, ordinary sensitivity.'

'No one of ordinary, normal –'

'– could –'

'– *write* a poem like that.'

'– have a –'

'– some kind of freak!'

'– bit of extra –'

'– *say* you were a freak. All I was –'

'– after classes, or –'

'– how you can do it!'

'I'll have them beans now,' said Danny, 'if you've finished.'

With a sigh, Kate pushed her plate across to him. When Ned and Vanessa got going nobody could get a word in. They were back on the same old boring subject. She heard Vanessa say, 'Do you realize you could actually be ordered to *drop* one of those things?'

Kate ate her raspberry crumble, drank her glass of skimmed milk, tried again. Quite loudly, addressing herself to Ned, she said: 'Do you think we could go over our scene again some time?'

Ned didn't even look at her. 'No way,' he said. 'No way!'

It took her a second or so to realize that he was saying it to Vanessa.

'So just tell me this!' Vanessa leaned forward across the table, her face close to Ned's. 'If they gave you the order, WHAT WOULD YOU DO?'

There was a silence. Ned sat frowning, making channels in a pool of spilt coffee.

'Well, answer me!' said Vanessa. She turned, for the first time to Kate and Danny. 'You see? He hasn't *got* any answer!'

'It's not that simple.'

'Are you telling me it's more simple to go and drop a bomb that would destroy half the world?'

Ned shook his head. 'That's not what I'm saying at all.'

'So what *are* you saying?'

'What I'm saying –'

Ned pushed his chair back. Vanessa pushed hers back. The next minute they had gone, marching out through the swing doors, locked in verbal combat. Kate wasn't sure that Ned had heard a single word she had said to him.

'Hey!' Danny reached across and tapped her on the back of the hand. 'I'll go over it with you, if you're really worried.'

'Would you?' She looked at him, gratefully. It wouldn't be the same as doing it with Ned, but at least it would be something.

They found an empty studio and ran the scene a couple of times. She had no difficulty with the lines: she had been word perfect for weeks.

'Want to do it for real?' said Danny.

'All right.'

It was strange, when she was still more than a little in awe of Ned and not in the least bit in awe of Danny, that she found it far easier to humble herself and act scared with him than she did with Ned. For the first time, it almost began to feel right.

'So what's the problem?'

'I don't seem to have one when I do it with you. Somehow, with Ned, it's – oh! I don't know.' She couldn't grouch to Danny about Ned; it wouldn't be fair. Not when they were flatmates. 'He just doesn't seem as – right as you do.'

'No, well –' Danny pulled a face. 'I've got a natural advantage, haven't I? Or disadvantage. Whichever way you care to look at it.'

'Oh, don't *you* start!' cried Kate.

'Start what?'

'Getting all heavy!'

'So what's heavy?'

'That poem you wrote –' Did he really feel that everyone that wasn't black was going round blaming everyone that was black for all the things that went wrong in society?

'She said to write something on things that you thought about. So those are some of the things that I think about.'

'But you don't actually *believe* it?' said Kate.

'Only sometimes.'

Only sometimes was bad enough. She looked at him, worried.

'You surely don't think – I mean, you surely don't –'

'No,' said Danny. 'Not really.'

But she knew now that he did. It was terrible how complex people were. Why couldn't they all be simple and straightforward like her? Life would be so much easier.

9

One evening, on television, they had a programme about the Falklands war. Kate normally didn't watch that sort of programme. Anything that was politics was bound to be boring. The only reason she watched this time was that she and Vanessa were round at the flat, *supposedly* rehearsing their scene from *Othello*, and that Vanessa wanted to. Everybody always had to do what Vanessa wanted – or so it sometimes seemed to Kate.

'You don't want to watch it, do you?' Danny asked Ned.

Ned shrugged a shoulder and said he didn't mind.

'I wouldn't have thought you would,' said Danny.

'Why not?' said Vanessa.

'You know what'll happen.'

'What will happen?'

'Nothing,' said Ned. 'Go on, turn it on.'

Danny shook his head. Kate said, 'What about the rehearsal?'

'How much rehearsal do you want?' Vanessa already was busily pressing buttons in search of the right channel. 'We've been at it nearly two hours. If it's not right now, it's never going to be.'

No. That was what Kate feared.

'It's not as bad as it was,' said Ned.

'Anyway, this is important. One can't live in a fantasy world *all* the time. One does occasionally have to look reality in the face.'

They looked reality in the face for about twenty minutes, then Danny jabbed Kate in the ribs and said, 'Fancy a pizza?'

There was a pizza bar just up the road where one large pizza and an extra large portion of chips was enough to feed four. They often ended the evening with one when they went round to Ned and Danny's. Kate turned, and jogged Vanessa.

'D'you feel like a –'

'Sh!' said Vanessa. She hated to be disturbed when she was concentrating.

'– pizza?' said Kate, switching her attention to Ned. Ned simply stuck up a thumb and went on watching.

Kate and Danny set off together.

'At least we get to choose,' said Kate. 'I vote cheese and tomato. And no olives. I loathe olives.' She usually gouged them out and handed them over to Vanessa. Well, tonight Vanessa could go without. If she couldn't even make the effort to be civil when a person spoke to her – 'She's seen *hundreds* of programmes on the Falklands. What's she want to see another one for?'

'Dunno why Ned wants to see it,' said Danny.

'Don't know why *any*body does.'

'Ned's old man was killed out there.'

'Ned's father?' Kate remembered, the night they had gone to the cinema, Ned saying that his father was dead. No wonder he hadn't wanted to talk about it. 'That's awful! And now he's *watching* it.'

'I guess some people are just gluttons for punishment.'

'P'raps he's hoping he might see him . . . was *he* in the army?'

'Yeah, some big high-up. Colonel, or something. I wouldn't want to see my old man on the box if he'd gone and got zeroed. Bit creepy, if you ask me.'

'Mm.' She supposed it was, a bit; though for years after her own father had died she had thought how wonderful it would be to have a video of him. Just to see how he had really been, as opposed to how she liked to think of him as being. But then, of course, her father hadn't been killed fighting a war. He had died of a heart attack. Actually, it was more romantic to die fighting in a war. She said so to Danny, as they turned into the pizza bar, but Danny said he couldn't see there was anything particularly romantic about it. He said he reckoned dying would be a pretty bum deal whichever way you went.

'But there are ways and ways,' urged Kate.

Danny said yes, and being shot through the head or blown up by a guided missile weren't either of the ways that he would choose.

'But for a cause,' she said.

Danny looked at her. 'What cause?'

'Well . . . it was something that had to be done.'

'Who said?'

'Oh, stop sounding like Vanessa! You know what I mean.'

'No, I don't,' said Danny.

'Yes, you do! You're just being difficult – like *her*.'

'Thing about Vanessa –' Danny broke off, briefly to place their order – 'cheese and tomato?'

'*Large*.'

'One large cheese and tomato and an extra large chips . . . thing about Vanessa, she might be a pain but she does talk sense. I mean, it *is* claptrap. All this guff they give you . . . all them loudmouths. *Politicians*. They're all the same. It's all a load of junk.'

'That's why I don't bother to think about it,' said

Kate. 'I just hope she isn't having a go at him.'

'Serve him right if she does. Anyone joins that lot needs their head examined.'

'You know something?' Kate stepped back a pace, looking up at him. 'You and Vanessa ought to get together . . . you're obviously made for each other.'

'You only say that 'cos you fancy Ned!' jeered Danny.

'I do not!'

' 'Course you do! Sticks out a mile.'

She felt her cheeks grow red. 'You're bonkers,' she said.

The Falklands programme, when they arrived back, had finished; either finished or been turned off. Vanessa was standing by the television, Ned still sitting on the sofa. Vanessa didn't actually say, 'What did you bother coming back for?' but Kate had the distinct feeling that she would like to have done. She had the feeling that they had interrupted something.

Just as well. She bet Vanessa had been having a go.

Their first class next morning was Movement, which they took with Group B. Ned didn't show, which Josh slyly suggested might have something to do with the fact that following Movement they had PD, and that Ned was now the only one who had not yet been called upon to do the Dreaded Letter Scene . . . 'Today'll be the day for sure!' Danny, however, said that Ned was in the building, he had just decided to cut Movement.

'Wow!' said Josh. 'He'll catch it. You wait till Morrison gets to hear!'

Mr Morrison, when it came to PD, was in a vile mood from the word go. He snapped at Josh to 'Sit up straight, for God's sake, and stop slumping! What are you trying to do? Give yourself curvature of the spine?' He told Vanessa to stop fiddling with her hair – 'We all know it's ravishing, you don't have to keep drawing attention to it' – and sarcastically asked Ned if he would be so kind as to desist from heavy breathing.

'You sound like some pervert making an obscene telephone call. What's the matter with you? You're not a smoker, are you?'

'No.' said Ned.

'Well, you sound like one. Anyone who smokes is a certifiable cretin.'

'I think I'm getting a cold,' said Ned.

'What's that supposed to be? Some kind of pre-emptive excuse? Get out there!' Mr Morrison jerked his thumb. 'Variation on the letter scene . . . you've been out of work for eighteen months. You're getting desperate. You keep writing off for jobs and ninety per cent of the people don't even bother to reply. This time, the worm has turned . . . you've actually fired off a broadside, complaining at the lack of manners. It brings a response. The response is an insult. Slap-in-the-face time. Give it to us!'

Ned coughed. 'You want me to read you the letter?'

'Yes. Get on with it. And *control that cough*.'

Mr Morrison really could be such a pig at times. Like Vanessa; *she* could be a pig. Kate looked thoughtfully from one to the other of them. Paul Morrison, with his blond hair and blue eyes and film star profile: Vanessa, with the sort of face that could melt a thousand ships, or whatever it was that faces did to ships. Maybe people with devastating good looks were always a bit piglike.

'What are we waiting for?' screamed Mr Morrison.

Kate saw Ned's jaw tighten. Instinctively, she felt

trouble looming. Ned would take a lot, but he wouldn't stand for being bullied. He had proved that with Vanessa. She did hope he wasn't going to do anything silly; not the mood Mr Morrison was in.

'OK.' Ned coughed again (people didn't cough on *purpose*) and from his pocket pulled an imaginary letter. 'I'll read it to you. "Dear Mr Carey – " ' He took a breath. His face was completely deadpan. ' "Thank you for your letter in which you complained of our failure to acknowledge yours of the first inst.

' "The fact is, however, that we are inundated with letters from unqualified little runts seeking to better themselves at our expense. Quite frankly we have neither the time nor the inclination to waste sending out replies.

' "In any case, our personnel officer, Mr Butcher, who would normally have responsibility for dealing with all the rubbish that pours in" ' (subdued giggle from Christine, hastily suppressed) ' "is temporarily out of action. On the very morning that your ludicrous whining drivel arrived, Mr Butcher had the great misfortune to be bitten on the fleshy part of the ear by a syphilitic parrot" ' (screech from Christine, snort from Sara) ' "flying in at the open window of his motor car as he was driving to the office. This, alas – " ' Ned, still straight-faced, turned the page – ' "caused him to swerve rather violently and crash his new Jaguar saloon into the back of a corporation dust cart" ' (more snorts) ' "with the result that he was forced to make the last few yards of his journey on foot, thus missing the lady with the coffee trolley. Thanks to his heroic efforts to catch up with it, going at speed across a polished floor" ' (collapse of Christine, followed swiftly by Sara and very nearly by Kate) ' "he has now ended up in hospital, where he has absolutely no desire to be pestered by miserable snivelling little gits such as yourself. I trust this satisfactorily answers your complaint.

"Wishing you every success for the future, I am, etc., etc. PS. Are you a Communist, or what?" '

Very solemnly, Ned folded the pages of his imaginary letter and put them back in his pocket. Kate's inside was aching with the effort of trying not to laugh. Danny was staring fixedly at the floor, Josh was chewing at a thumb nail. Sara hiccuped and wiped a finger beneath her eyes. Christine was bent double. Vanessa alone seemed unaffected.

'End of letter,' said Ned.

There was a pause.

This is awful, thought Kate. He's going to be flayed.

'WHAT THE HELL DO YOU THINK YOU'RE PLAYING AT?'

The words went roaring round the room, blasting off the walls, off the windows, off the furniture. Christine abruptly sat up straight; Josh took his finger out of his mouth. Danny went on staring at the floor. Kate had to force herself to look at Ned. To her surprise, he was meeting Mr Morrison's gaze quite squarely and steadily. She didn't know how he dared.

'You said you wanted it to be an insult.'

'Yes, and it *was* a bloody insult! An insult to me, an insult to your fellow students! You know damned well what I gave you that scene for! I thought you could at least manage to express anger – at least express *some*thing. But oh, no! We have to play Mr Cool, Mr Smoothie, Mr Smartmouth! Never do anything that might get us into a bit of a lather. Life's just one big yawn to you, isn't it?'

Ned looked at him, but said nothing.

'Well? Cat got your tongue?' Mr Morrison's face, which was normally quite smooth and pale, had become alarmingly mottled. His blue eyes bulged dementedly. 'What is it with you? In all the time you've been here you haven't learnt one damned thing . . . You pull out the stops for about five seconds, then we're straight back to square one, playing everything as if you've got a poker stuck up your arse! Well, I am here to tell you,' said Mr Morrison, 'that nobody wings through *this* course on the strength of a pretty face. If you're not willing to give, then as far as I'm concerned you can go. Because I am just not interested. I'm in this job to help people open out, not clam up. I'm giving you due warning . . . either you pull your finger out and start producing the goods, or I've had it with you. Which is it to be?'

Ned swallowed; still he said nothing.

'WHAT THE HELL ARE WE TO DO WITH YOU?' Mr Morrison spun round, suddenly, to confront the rest of the class. 'What's your suggestion? What makes him tick? There's got to be one thing, just *one* thing, he can get worked up about! Come on, I need your help! Give me some ideas.'

Everyone, for some reason, looked at Vanessa; but Vanessa, like Ned, said nothing. It was unlike her to be bereft of ideas. Kate racked her brains. What *did* make Ned tick? It was Danny, in the end, who came up with something. She saw him take out his rough book, scribble a few words, hand it to Mr Morrison.

'What's this?' Mr Morrison frowned as he read it. His brow cleared. 'Yes! Why not? We'll give it a go. All of you – up! Make the chairs into a barricade. Come on, come on, look sharp! Scene is, that's a missile site. He's on duty, guarding it. You're all part of a demo . . . CND, peace people, what you will. I want you to taunt him – hurl abuse at him. Feel free. Let rip. Lay it on with a trowel. What the hell is all that racket about?'

Mr Morrison strode to the door. Outside, Group B were gathered, shrieking and yelling as usual as they waited their turn to come in. Christine took the opportunity to say, 'I don't believe in CND. I think they're just agitators. We *need* nuclear weapons.'

'Yeah, like we need AIDS,' said Danny.

Mr Morrison came back into the room, followed by the mob that were Group B.

'Reinforcements! Now you can all have a go at him. I want him rattled – I want him provoked! *I want him broken!* Get to it.'

For just a second, there was silence. They stood, self-conscious, looking at Ned on the other side of the chairs. Kate tried to imagine how it would be if he were a real soldier, wearing uniform, carrying a gun. Mr Morrison must have had the same thought, for he suddenly snatched a ruler from out of his desk drawer and thrust it at Ned across the barricade. Ned took it, but seemed bewildered.

'Come on, come on!' Mr Morrison snapped his fingers. 'Look to it, soldier! You want a weapon, don't you? Not going to face a howling mob unarmed!'

It was Judy, little fat Judy, who set the ball rolling.

'Murderer!' she cried. She shook her fist in Ned's face. 'That's what you lot are . . . murderers!'

'Capitalist lackeys!'

'Tools of the Establishment!'

'Don't you *care*? Don't you *think*?'

'You ought to be ashamed of yourself!'

Group B were the most vociferous. It seemed that not being as close to Ned as the members of his own group, they found it easier to abuse him.

'What are you going to do, soldier, when the order's given?'

'Are you going to be the one that presses the button?'

'Or are you going to run for it?'

'Where's he going to run to?'

'Oh, soldier man, where you gonna run to?' Someone – Danny, probably – started the refrain, the others swiftly took it up. Soon the whole mob was chanting it:

Oh, soldier man, where you gonna run to
Oh, soldier man, where you gonna run to
All on that day?
Run from the light
Satan's gonna see you
Run from the light –

The only person not singing was Vanessa. She was practically tone deaf, but that wouldn't normally have stopped her. Normally she would have been right up there, at the barricades, singing the loudest, shouting the hardest. Today, Kate couldn't remember hearing her shout anything at all. She turned to look at her, and as she did so the mob surged forward, carrying Kate with them. They were going over! Judy and Sara – *Sara* – had jumped on to the chairs and were screaming at Ned over the top of them, threatening to jump.

'Well, what are you waiting for?' shouted Mr Morrison. 'You've got a weapon – use it!'

Ned hesitated. He took a step backwards.

'Hey, soldier!' taunted Sara. 'Big brave soldier with his big brave gun . . . are you going to shoot us, soldier?'

'Just don't come any closer,' said Ned.

'Why not? What are you scared of?'

'What are you scared of, soldier boy? Scared we'll come and steal your bomb away?'

Someone in the mob, for by now it really was a mob, lobbed a book across the barricades. It hit Ned in the chest and bounced off. Soon all manner of objects were flying through the air – purses, hair brushes, even a tube of toothpaste. The floor on the other side of the barricade began to look like a battle-field.

'I'm coming over!' shrieked Sara.

She jumped.

'*FIRE!*' roared Mr Morrison.

Sara froze. The mob stilled and was silent. Ned took a breath.

They waited.

'I said fire!' bawled Mr Morrison. '*That was an order . . . FIRE!*'

Ned stood, shoulders hunched. His face, always pale, had turned sheet white. A film of perspiration beaded his upper lip. He breathed painfully.

And still they waited.

Suddenly, from the back, came Vanessa's voice, light and sharp: 'Well, soldier boy? What you gonna do?'

It was plainly a challenge. Kate saw the muscles in Ned's face twitch. He raised his arm. For a few taut seconds she genuinely thought he was going to fire; then slowly, very slowly, his arm fell back, the ruler clattered to the floor, Ned choked and was gone.

Vanessa was the first to move, carving a path through the suddenly subdued crowd.

'Where do you think you're going?' snarled Mr Morrison.

'I'm going to see if N –'

'Leave him!'

'But he –'

'I said, leave him!'

Not even Vanessa dared defy Mr Morrison. Mutinously, she came back into the room.

'Right! Get this lot cleared. Has anyone in Group A got a class they're supposed to be at?'

Christine said she had a French class which had

started fifteen minutes ago. She was allowed to leave; the rest were told to stay. They listened as she clumped down the stairs on her plaster cast. Vanessa, still looking mutinous, helped hump the chairs back into place. The others picked up their scattered belongings. Nobody seemed to know what to say, or where to look, reluctant to risk even a quick glance for fear of catching another's eye.

'I feel terrible,' said Sara, 'doing that to Ned.'

'I don't see why,' said Mr Morrison. 'It was a valuable experience for him – for all of you. Demonstrated just how easy it is to be carried away by group emotion.'

Vanessa tossed her head. 'Group *hysteria*.'

'So? It served its purpose.'

They had broken Ned, which was what he had wanted.

'Shall I go and see if he's OK?' said Danny.

'Why shouldn't he be OK? His psyche's not that frail, is it?' Kate thought, but couldn't be sure, that she saw Danny and Vanessa exchange glances. 'If he can't survive a little emotional contretemps he's got no right to be here!'

Only when the room had been restored to some semblance of normality, with approximately five minutes of Group B's session still left, did Mr Morrison turn to Kate and say, 'OK! Since you're all so worried . . . go and find him and tell him I want a word.'

'I'll go,' said Vanessa.

'You will not go! I asked Trottie. You can stay here.'

Vanessa flushed. 'But we're supposed to be having our break!'

'You can have your break afterwards. Go on, Trottie, off you go.'

All very well saying find Ned, but there were at

least a dozen places where he could be. She tried them all, without success, finally nerving herself to ask John Durrant, as he came out of the boys' cloakroom, if Ned were in there. Kate was secretly a bit afraid of John Durrant. He stalked aggressively and wore his hair in dreadlocks. Judy said he was gorgeous, and Kate supposed he was, but he had a way of looking at you which made you feel that white was definitely inferior. (Vanessa, perversely, said that that just showed how racist she was – 'If you weren't, it wouldn't occur to you.' Vanessa was always so contrary.)

Rather to Kate's surprise, John Durrant didn't stalk past as if she weren't there (let alone spit in her face and call her a honky bitch, which was what she always half expected.) He said, 'Seen him heading that way,' and gestured towards the main admin block. Over his shoulder, as he walked off, he added: 'Not looking so good.'

'Oh?'

Kate hurried on, down the corridor. She supposed that after an ordeal such as Ned had just gone through, a person probably wouldn't look too good. He hadn't been looking all that good to begin with. He was obviously suffering from a cold and feeling rotten. Mr Morrison really was such a *pig*.

She reached the end of the corridor and stopped. What would Ned be coming to the admin block for? There wasn't anything there – well, only Studio 6. Studio 6 was where he had gone that other time, with Vanessa, when they had wanted to be private and have their row. Students still weren't allowed in there: there was still a barrier across the corridor and a large notice which said NO ENTRY. It would be the perfect place for retiring to lick wounds.

She wondered if it was worth taking a chance. No one was about. She might as well.

'Ned?' Gingerly (because who knew? The real reason for putting it out of bounds might be that the Principal liked to go there and snog) she pushed open the door.

Somebody was in there. She could make out a shadowy figure, hunched over a chair. The reason the figure was shadowy was that there wasn't a great deal of light coming into the room. Boards had been nailed across the windows and steel joists held up the ceiling.

'Ned?' whispered Kate.

Was it Ned? Nervously, on tiptoe, she crept further in. It *was* Ned. But what was he doing? *Crying?*

No! Ned wouldn't cry; boys didn't. At least, she didn't think they did.

'Ned?' she whispered. 'Are you all right?'

He wasn't. She could see that he wasn't. She could *hear* that he wasn't. Suddenly she thought: he's having a heart attack!

Panic swept through her. What did one do for heart attacks? Sit people up, lie people down, call for a doctor –

Call for a doctor! Kate turned, and fled. In her blind haste she tripped over the barrier and bashed her knee cap. Then, as she hobbled round the corner, she crashed into Vanessa, coming the other way. Vanessa grabbed her.

'Where is he?'

'He's in there, but –'

'Is he OK?'

'No, he's not, I think he's –'

Vanessa didn't wait to hear any more. She was off and away, down the passage, ducking under the NO ENTRY sign, unceremoniously bursting through the door into Studio 6. Kate floundered in her wake.

'I think we ought to get someone, I think he's having a heart attack, I think –'

'Of course he's not having a heart attack!' Vanessa rounded on her, fiercely. 'Don't be so ridiculous! Just go away and leave him to me.'

'But –'

'Trottie, will you just *do as I tell you*?'

'But I –'

'*GO*!' said Vanessa. 'And don't you dare to blab to anyone!'

Immensely offended, Kate took herself off. In silent dignity, she limped back up the corridor. If Ned died, it would be entirely Vanessa's fault.

On her way back up to Room 4.4, to report to Mr Morrison, she bumped into Danny.

'Did you find him?'

'Yes, but *she*'s with him. She sent me away. *I* think he needs a doctor. I think he's ill.' It was a relief to tell Danny, even though Vanessa had told her not to blab. (Who was Vanessa, anyway? What right had she to lay down the law?) Telling Danny at least removed some of the burden from Kate's shoulders. If *he* thought they should get a doctor –

'Nah,' said Danny. 'He'll come through it. Come and have some lunch.'

Kate stared. She had never thought that Danny would be callous. 'Don't you *care*?'

'Yeah, I think it's dead rough, but since there's nothing we can actually do –'

'We could call a doctor!'

'And get clobbered for our pains.'

'So who cares about that?'

'I do,' said Danny.

'Well, I don't!' said Kate. She pushed past him.

'Where you going?'

'I'm going to *find* someone and *tell* them.'

'He won't like it.'

Kate hesitated, half turned. 'Why not?'

' 'Cos he won't.'

'Why?'

' 'Cos he's dead against it.'

'Why?'

' 'Cos –' Danny lowered his voice. 'He'll kill me for this . . .'cos he gets asthma, see, and –'

'Asthma?' A girl at the Nunnery had had asthma. Gillian Beadle. Sometimes she had had it so badly she couldn't even walk across the room. *'Ned?'*

'Yeah. When he gets into a state about something . . . brings it on. 's why he tries not to get too worked up.'

'You mean it's happened before? You mean, you *knew*?'

'Yeah – well – be hard not to, wouldn't it? Living with the guy.'

'So in that case –' Kate was suddenly indignant. (Indignant, partly, at having been made to look a fool . . . *I think he's having a heart attack* . . . how Vanessa would jeer!) 'What did you want to go and suggest that horrible scene for? If you knew what it would do to him? What – ?'

She stopped. Vanessa had known, too. How come she had known and not Kate?

'See, what it was,' said Danny, 'way I saw it –'

Kate listened with half an ear as Danny earnestly explained how he hadn't suggested the scene on purpose to make Ned ill, he'd suggested it in the hope of helping, in the hope of averting the further wrath of Mr Morrison, and anyway it was partly Ned's own fault for watching that stupid programme last night, Danny had tried to stop him, Kate had been there, she had *seen* him try to stop him. Anyone could have told him it was asking for trouble, watching a programme about a war in which his old man had been killed, but he would do it, he had to go and titillate himself, he had to –

'Does Vanessa know about his father being killed?'

'I dunno. Dunno what she knows.'

She'd known about him having asthma. She could understand Danny knowing. After all, as he said, he lived under the same roof. But *Vanessa* –

'I do think someone might have told me,' said Kate. 'I was really scared in there just now. I really thought he was having a heart attack.'

'Yeah, me, too,' said Danny. 'That first time – time he lost his rag with Vanessa. That time she came round and started on at him, 'bout the army. D'you remember?'

'Yes.' Kate remembered. Ned and Vanessa had gone at it hammer and tongs till almost midnight. She and Vanessa had missed their last train and had to get a minicab.

'Frightened the life out me,' said Danny. 'Never thought he'd last the night, never mind make it into class next day.'

'That was the day he was late and Morrison got mad at him.' The day he hadn't wanted to fence and Miss Dando had told him not to be so feeble. Suddenly, looking back, a whole lot of things began falling into place. Ned joking, saying he really must stop smoking so heavily; Ned, after *Streetcar*, after he and Vanessa had torn strips off each other – and *that* was all Vanessa's fault. She was the one who had started it.

'Anyway,' said Danny, 'so long as he's got someone with him –'

Vanessa. Who'd want Vanessa?

'– we might just as well go to lunch. 'Cos honestly, you call a doctor, he'll do his nut.' He looked at Kate, hopefully. 'You coming?'

'I've just got to go and see Morrison. What shall I tell him?'

'Tell him you couldn't find him?'

'Or shall I tell him the truth?'

There was a pause.

'If I told him,' said Kate, 'it might stop him getting mad at him all the time.'

Danny seemed doubtful.

'Well, it might,' said Kate. After all, Ned could hardly be yelled at for getting asthma. It was hardly his fault.

Danny shrugged. 'Up to you. See you in the refectory.'

Kate continued slowly up the stairs to Mr Morrison's room. Vanessa had told her not to blab. *Don't you dare to blab to anyone!* Who did Vanessa think she was, issuing her orders? Kate would do whatever she decided was best.

10

Vanessa was going to be furious. Kate knew she was and she didn't care. She just *didn't care*. She had done what she thought was right. It wasn't her fault if Mr Morrison had gone marching down to Studio 6 to see Ned for himself. It wasn't her fault if Vanessa had been sent packing. She had a class at twelve-thirty and Mr Morrison had told her to go to it. He had then sought out Danny and Kate in the refectory and asked them whether they intended going straight home after classes, and if so whether they would be responsible for seeing that Ned got back safely.

'I don't want him going on his own. Can I rely on you? I'll call a cab, so you won't have to bother with buses. What time do you finish?'

Danny finished at three-fifteen, so did Kate. Vanessa didn't finish until almost five o'clock. Kate left a note for her, pinned to her locker: HAVE GONE BACK TO THE FLAT WITH NED AND DANNY. SEE YOU LATER. She was going to be absolutely *furious*.

Ned was waiting for them in the lounge.

'What's this?' he said. 'A deputation? Hi, Trottie.'

'We've come to take you home,' said Kate. 'We've got a cab outside. Mr Morrison called it – *and* he's paid for it.'

'Wow! Star treatment.'

'How you feeling?' said Danny.

'How am I looking?'

Danny considered him, critically. 'Rough.'

'So that's how I'm feeling.'

'It's your own fault. You would ins –'

'I know, I know!'

'I told you not to watch that poxy programme. Didn't I? Didn't I tell you? And you had to go and do it.'

'It was Vanessa's fault,' said Kate. 'She was the one that turned it on.'

'That's right,' said Ned. 'It was the Harridan's fault. You tell her.'

'I will,' said Kate.

On their way out of the building, walking slowly because Ned didn't have much breath to spare, they passed John Durrant. He said, 'I see you found him, then.'

'Was someone looking for me?' said Ned.

'Earlier,' said Kate. 'Mr Morrison wanted you.'

'Oh.'

Kate hesitated. 'You didn't mind,' she said, 'about me telling him?'

Ned waited until they were outside. 'I guess it doesn't really make much difference.'

'It's just that I had to tell him something. And it only seemed sensible. I mean, he was quite nice about it really, wasn't he? Once he knew. Calling a cab and all. And he didn't bawl you out again, did he?' Ned shook his head. 'I knew he wouldn't, once he knew. And he would have had to know, sooner or later. I mean –'

Ned was holding the cab door for her. That was typical of Ned: nice manners. Even when he was ill. She beamed at him. It wasn't really something you could hide from people was what she had been about to say, but perhaps Ned mightn't like that. Perhaps he thought it *was* something you could hide from people though she really couldn't think why he should want to. Gillian Beadle hadn't tried to hide it. In fact, Gillian Beadle had gone round telling everyone who could be persuaded to listen. 'My Asthma' she used to call it, as it it were some special mark of distinction. Of course, Ned was a more private sort of person than Gillian Beadle; she could quite understand that he mightn't want to shout about it. On the other hand, it wasn't anything to be ashamed of. Or maybe he thought it was. It was difficult to tell, with Ned.

'You'd have got into the most awful row,' she said, 'cutting Movement.'

'I'd have thought up some excuse.'

'You'd still have got into a row.'

Ned shrugged, as if to say he was used to getting into rows.

'Beats me,' said Danny, 'why he had to go and watch the poxy thing in the first place. Just *stupid*. What you go and do it for?'

Ned shook his head.

'Don't go on at him,' said Kate.

'Well, but it's asking for trouble, in't it? Almost like doing it on purpose. I mean, what's the point of deliberately going and making yourself ill?'

'For your information –' Ned spoke with dignity, albeit with some difficulty – 'I did not – deliberately – set out – to make myself – ill.'

'So what d'you *do* it for?'

'Oh –' Ned waved a hand, as if the effort of explaining himself were too much. 'Just because.'

'Stupid rubbishing programme. Dragging it all up again.'

'It was Vanessa,' said Kate.

'She wasn't – to know.'

'No! But you was,' said Danny.

'She always gets so *angry*,' said Kate. 'Anyone crosses her –'

There was a pause. Ned took an inhaler from his pocket. Gillian Beadle had had an inhaler. She had always been losing it, then panicking in moments of crisis.

'Have you always had asthma?' said Kate.

'Mm.'

'*Al*ways?'

'Not – always.'

'I knew someone had it really badly.'

'Don't go giving him ideas,' said Danny.

'This girl at school . . . Gillian Beadle. She had to go and have tests and things. Find out why she got it.'

'He knows why he gets it. Watches these –'

'Belt up!' Kate jabbed at Danny with her elbow. She turned sympathetically to Ned. 'You could be allergic to something.' Gillian Beadle had been allergic to dust. The trouble with dust was, you couldn't really get away from it.'

'He's not allergic!' said Danny.

'How do you know?' Ned lay back and closed his eyes. 'I could well be allergic . . . to people going on at me!'

If that were the case, thought Kate, he would be super-allergic to Vanessa. I wouldn't go on at him, she thought. Vanessa was notoriously unsympathetic. She had never had the least bit of patience with Gillian Beadle. To be honest, Kate hadn't had that much, either, but then Gillian Beadle had been a pain, forever whining and seeking attention. Ned didn't do either of those things.

As the cab rounded a corner, his head fell against her shoulder. Kate sat, frozen into position, scarcely daring to draw breath in case she disturbed him. She couldn't see Vanessa letting Ned rest his head on her shoulder. (She couldn't see Ned *wanting* to.) If Danny hadn't been there she might have been brave enough to put an arm round him, but she couldn't in front of Danny. It would embarrass her too much. Already he was grinning.

'Aow, wot a luvly pickcher!' Danny put both hands beneath his cheek and made a snoring sound. Ned immediately opened his eyes.

'Where are we?' He raised his head. 'Are we there?'

'Not yet,' said Kate, but he didn't put his head back. Danny, the beast, just grinned even more.

Ned's grandmother's flat was quite large. It had three bedrooms (one with its own bathroom and dressing-room), two sitting rooms, a dining-room, kitchen and bath; but most of it – what Ned called 'the Granny area' – was kept closed for much of the year, only being opened up when Ned's grandmother came back from Malta or his mother wanted to stay in London to do her research or see publishers.

The part that Ned and Danny lived in was just four small rooms – bedroom, sitting-room, kitchen and bath. Every single one of them was what Kate's mother would have called 'a midden'. A midden to Kate's mother was dirty water in the sink, dirty dishes on the draining board, remnants of the past week's meals on the kitchen table, unmade beds in the bedroom, and clothes stacked high on every available surface.

Kate, whose own bedroom qualified permanently as a midden, and who agreed wholeheartedly with Vanessa that housework was a job fit only for morons, now with much fretting and tutting set about the task of clearing up after two able-bodied males perfectly capable of clearing up after themselves. She made the excuse that just at this moment Ned *wasn't* able-bodied; if he had been, she wouldn't have lifted so much as a finger. To be fair to Danny, he did help her. He grumbled – 'Dunno what we're doing this for' – but he did it. When the place was spotless (by Kate's standards if not her mother's), Kate said she would make a cup of tea.

'Don't think there is any,' said Danny.

'Well, coffee, then.'

Danny said he didn't think there was any of that, either. He said both he and Ned were broke. Until Danny got paid on Saturday for his Saturday job they didn't have more than their bus fares and a few odd pence between them.

'So what are you living on?' said Kate.

Danny said porridge, mostly – porridge and pizza.

'But that's awful! You'll get malnutritioned.'

'Nah, nice plate of porridge, does you good.'

It didn't look as if it had done Ned much good, thought Kate.

'Porridge the way I make it . . . expert porridge-maker, I am. One cuppa water, one cuppa milk –'

'Have you got any milk?'

Danny said yes, they had some of that.

'Very well, then! I shall make hot milk.'

'But I can't stand hot milk!'

'I wasn't thinking of you,' said Kate. 'I was thinking of Ned.'

'What's he want hot milk for?'

She wasn't quite sure, except that when people were ill you gave them hot drinks. Her mother had always given her and Vanessa hot drinks when they had been in bed with anything. Usually it had been lemon barley or blackcurrant cordial, but now and again it had been hot milk.

She had to use a burnt porridge pan. All the pans had burnt porridge in them. (She didn't think that Danny could be terribly good at making porridge, in spite of his grandiose claim.) Danny watched in fascination as she poured the heated milk into a coffee mug and prepared to take it through to Ned in the sitting room.

'This I have to see!'

Of course there would be a battle; she knew that. Everyone staged battles over hot milk. She and Vanessa had always screamed the place down. (Vanessa once, in an act of revenge, had actually managed to sick hers up all over a clean duvet cover.) Kate would stand for no nonsense, however. This was the first time she had ever really been on her own with Danny and Ned, ie: *without Vanessa*, and she found that she was enjoying it. She began to wonder whether she had missed her vocation – whether perhaps she should have gone into nursing. She had a sudden pleasing vision of herself, wearing a frilly cap and starched apron, tending bedfuls of young men all handsomely and romantically ill with diseases which might take them to their graves but would never actually disfigure them.

'Drink up!' she said.

Ned looked round, in astonishment, at Danny. 'She can't be serious?'

'I think she is,' said Danny.

'Do you good,' urged Kate.

'Trottie, you can't do this to me! I'm not well!'

'Make you feel better,' said Kate.

'Drinkie, drinkie,' said Danny. 'There's a good boy. Want me to hold him for you?'

'Thank you,' said Kate. 'Violence will not be necessary. He's going to drink it nicely, aren't you?' A power surge came over her. 'You are,' she said, 'aren't you?'

'You are,' said Danny, 'aren't you?'

'But I loathe hot milk!'

'So do I,' said Danny.

'So why should I have to drink the filthy muck?'

' 'Cos you was a silly boy,' said Danny. 'You

went and watched a programme what you didn't ought to have watched and now you got to pay the price.'

'Drink it before it gets cold,' said Kate.

'Trottie, I shall never forgive you for this.' Ned held out a hand for the mug. 'I shall nurture grudges as long as I live.'

'That's all right,' said Kate.

She wasn't feeling shy any more. She had thought, just recently, that she might be tongue-tied if she were to be alone with Ned in the flat for any length of time. Now she found herself wishing that Danny had something else to do, something that would take him away, so that it could be just her and Ned. She wondered if she had enough money in her purse to suggest that he went down the road and bought a pizza. She had just decided that she had when the doorbell rang. Danny went off to answer it. Almost at once, they heard Vanessa's voice: 'Is Trottie still here?'

'The Harridan!' said Ned. 'That's all I need!'

It was all anyone needed. They had been getting on so well! Kate and Danny had cleaned the flat, Ned was drinking his milk, Danny had been about to go up the road for a pizza – what did Vanessa have to come and ruin everything for? Who wanted her? Who had asked her?

Vanessa was so *bossy*. She could never be anywhere without taking over. First she picked up Ned's empty coffee mug and sniffed at it and said, 'Ugh! *Milk?* Milk clogs your tubes, you oughtn't to be drinking milk.' And then she said, 'Why aren't you in bed? I should have thought you ought to be resting.' And then, 'For goodness' sake! It's like an oven in here. I'm surprised you can breathe at *all*.' Finally, she had the nerve to suggest that Kate – *Kate!* – went down the road to get a pizza.

Kate said, 'Why should I go? Why can't you?'

'I only just got here,' said Vanessa.

'So you could have picked one up on your way!'

'Didn't know if we'd want one, did I? Might want something different.'

Ned said he didn't want anything at all. Danny said they hadn't any money anyway. Kate said that she was sick of pizzas. In the end, nobody went anywhere for anything.

They sat around for a bit, sharing a can of Coke which Danny had managed to unearth from a pile of old tins beneath the kitchen sink, but the evening never really took off. Danny was the only one at his ease. Ned was in no fit state for talking, and there was definite tension between Kate and Vanessa. They left at seven-thirty: the row started the minute they hit the pavement.

'You might have called me!' snapped Vanessa.

'Called you what?' Nosy, bossy, interfering cow?

'Called me out of class!'

'What for?'

'So I could have come back with him, of course!'

'Why should he want you to c –'

'Because I know what to do,' said Vanessa, 'and you quite obviously don't.'

She liked her cheek! What had Vanessa done when she had got there other than bully and nag and order people about?

'*Fussing* at him. He can't stand people fussing at him! He just likes to be left alone till he gets over it.'

She couldn't see Vanessa leaving anyone alone. And anyway, she resented the accusation of fussing.

'I was not fussing! I –'

'Giving him *milk* to drink.' Vanessa's voice was full of contempt. 'Everyone knows that milk's bad for chest complaints!'

Since when?

'It clogs up the tubes. It –'

'So you said!'

'So what did you give it to him for?'

'Because it was all there was!' screamed Kate.

'So why give him anything? Why couldn't you just *leave* him?'

'You didn't just leave him, that time after Duologues!'

'I stayed with him. I didn't *fuss*. And what do you know about it? I suppose you were spying?'

'Yes, I was!' shrilled Kate. 'Spying through the keyhole with a big telescope! That's what you'd like to think, isn't it? Think you're so interesting, so beautiful, so *wonderful*, no one can keep their eyes off you! If you must know, you were making such a racket, bawling and yelling –'

'Just like you are now! And I wasn't bawling and yelling at him *after*wards, I was bawling at him *before* –'

'Upsetting him,' shrieked Kate, 'before a performance! When you *knew*!'

'I didn't know, you stupid cow! I wouldn't have done it if I'd known, would I?'

'I don't see why not, it hasn't stopped you doing it since. I suppose you had another go at him last night, after that programme! And *that* was all your fault. Making him watch the horrid thing.'

'He didn't have to if he didn't want.'

'So what's he supposed to do? Go into another room?'

'He could have turned it off.'

'Oh, yes? And you'd have let him? All that junk about *facing up to reality* . . . Did you know,' screeched Kate, 'that Ned's father was *killed* in the Falklands?'

'He told me.'

'He *told* you?'

'After we'd watched it.'

'You mean, after you'd gone on at him!'

'I wouldn't have gone on at him if he'd told me before, but it still doesn't make any difference to the way I feel. I'd still tell him how I felt. I'd tell anyone how I felt.'

'Yes, don't we know!' said Kate.

'All right, motor mouth! If we're going to start hurling accusations, why did you have to go and blab to Morrison after I'd told you not to?'

'Why shouldn't I blab to Morrison? What am I supposed to say to him?'

'You didn't have to tell him about Ned having asthma!'

'Why not? Why shouldn't I?'

'Because he'd rather you didn't, that's why!'

'Well, how am I supposed to know? If nobody *tells* me anything?'

'That's just the reason people don't tell you anything, because you can't keep your big mouth shut!'

It seemed to Kate there was a logical flaw here somewhere, but by now she was too cross to stop and work it out.

'It's all your fault, anyway,' she said. 'If you didn't keep going on at him all the time he probably wouldn't get it. Not as much. Not as *badly*. Talk about people not keeping their big mouths shut . . . I think you're rotten! All he wants to do is go into the army and be a soldier like his father. Why can't you just shut up and leave him alone?'

'Oh, belt up, Trottie! You don't know what you're talking about. You don't understand . . . you never understand anything!'

By the time they reached home they were no longer talking. Vanessa stormed up to her bedroom, Kate stumped into the sitting-room. The television was on, though nobody seemed to be watching it.

Kate's mother was playing some complicated game of Patience, laying out the cards face down all over the table. Vanessa's father had his headphones on and was listening to music. They weren't talking, either; they very rarely did. Kate sometimes looked at them and wondered why they had ever got married. What was in it for *them*? There was certainly nothing in it for her and Vanessa.

Jacko, lying on the hearth rug, slowly opened a rheumy eye and wagged his motheaten tail. Kate rushed across and hugged him. She often thought that Jacko was the only thing in life worth living for.

11

The trouble with Vanessa was that just as you'd come to a firm decision to hate her she went and did something which made hatred quite impossible: she went and made you grateful. It was terrible having to feel gratitude to a person who only a short while ago you had wanted to pummel into senselessness. But how could you not, when she'd gone and saved the only thing in your life worth living for?

Every day before breakfast Kate took Jacko for his walk in the park. When Jacko had been young he had been a fighter, but he was an old dog now and he didn't look for trouble. That morning, on the way back up the road, only four doors from home, trouble found him. It came in the shape of a large black dog, off the lead (which it shouldn't have been) full of bumptiousness and spoiling for a fight.

The black dog took one look at Jacko and sprang. Kate screamed and hauled on Jacko's lead, half throttling him. The owner of the black dog did nothing at all. He called, 'Boney! Leave!' but Boney took no notice. He had his teeth sunk into Jacko's ruff and was shaking him, to and fro, like a rat. Kate screamed and screamed. Boney's owner shouted 'BONEY! LEAVE!' but he didn't risk going near.

Kate was almost beside herself. The black dog had dragged Jacko halfway across the road. Jacko, fighting bravely, didn't stand a chance. He was too old, too frail, too toothless.

'Jacko!' shrieked Kate. The tears streamed down her cheeks. Jacko was being shaken to death in front of her eyes and there was not a thing that anyone could do to stop it. Never interfere in a dog fight; wasn't that what they said? 'Oh, Jacko,' whimpered Kate.

Suddenly, a door slammed. A figure came flying down the garden path, leaped the garden gate, tore into the road like a virago, roaring and flailing its arms.

'STOP THAT!'

Vanessa's voice must have been heard several streets away. She cuffed the black dog about the head, roundly, like a mother administering a slap to a naughty child. The black dog, surprised, paused for just a second. A second was long enough. Kate sprang forward, gathering Jacko to her. Vanessa grabbed Boney by the collar. (Vanessa didn't even *like* dogs; not really. Not the way Kate did.)

Boney's owner stepped forward. He was wearing a white shirt with a stripy tie and a neat grey suit.

'Bad boy,' he said, and put the black dog on his lead. Then he shook his head reproachfully at Vanessa. 'Shouldn't have done that,' he said. 'Much better just let them fight it out.'

'Idiot,' said Vanessa, as he walked away. 'Well, come on, then!' She turned, impatient, to Kate. 'Don't sit there grizzling over him, let's get him back indoors!'

With the tears still flowing, Kate scooped Jacko into her arms and staggered the few yards with him to the house. If anything should happen to Jacko –

'Let's have a look! Put him on his chair, so we can see.'

It was Vanessa who examined him, Vanessa who discovered the puncture marks in his neck where the black dog had held him: Kate who bathed his wounds, wrapped him in a blanket, tenderly settled him back on his chair. Scarcely two seconds later he was on his hind legs at the kitchen window, barking defiance at next-door's cat. As Vanessa said, there couldn't be too much wrong. Kate's mother promised she would take him down to the vet later on, but it was really only a precautionary measure, in case of the bite turning septic.

'Fuss, fuss, fuss,' said Vanessa, but she didn't say it nastily, and as they left the house she actually gave Jacko a bit of a pat, which was something she almost never did. 'Stupid old rat bag!' she said. It was one of those rare moments when Kate felt a real surge of affection for Vanessa.

As they walked up to the bus stop together there was a closeness between them which had not been there for a long time. Hard to remember that only twelve hours ago they had been consumed with bitterness and loathing.

'Just as well you were there,' said Kate. 'That man wasn't doing a *thing*.'

In another mood Vanessa might have pointed out that Kate hadn't been doing that much, either. Today all she said was, 'I saw you from my bedroom window. I thought if someone didn't do something we'd end up with a dead dog and then you'd have gone all daft and weepy.'

'Yes, I would,' said Kate. It wasn't something she would always have admitted, but she didn't mind today.

'I couldn't stand to have *two* walking disasters on my hands.'

'Two? said Kate.

'Ned.'

'Oh.' She thought for a while about Ned. She thought of that terrible moment in Studio 6 when she had been convinced he was having a heart attack. And what had she done? Nothing! Nothing for Ned, nothing for Jacko. Just wrung her hands and panicked. Vanessa might be bossy and self-opinionated, but at least she took action in emergencies. She couldn't see Vanessa just wringing her hands and panicking. 'You know that other time,' she said. 'That time after *Streetcar* . . . was he as bad then as he was yesterday?'

'He was quite bad. Not *as* bad.'

'Did you think he was having a heart attack?'

'No,' said Vanessa. 'I thought he was having asthma . . . I thought of Gillian Beadle.'

'Oh.' Why hadn't Kate thought of Gillian Beadle?

'I remembered her using her inhaler – d'you remember, she was always losing it?'

Kate nodded, dumbly.

'Always leaving it in stupid places . . . in the showers, or on the hockey field, or something. Mind you, Ned's almost as bad. He'd left his in his locker. You should have seen their faces when I went bursting in! John Durrant was there, I thought he was going to murder me.' Vanessa paused. 'Did you know you've gone bright scarlet?'

'Have I?' said Kate.

'Yes –' A wicked gleam suddenly appeared in Vanessa's eye. 'That's been really bothering you, hasn't it? It's been really getting at you!'

'It hasn't been getting at me, it's just –'

'Just that you've been half dead of vulgar curiosity! *I* know what's been going through your nasty little mind!'

Kate's cheeks flared. 'It wasn't me,' she said. 'It was Danny.'

'That's right, blame someone else!'

'Well, it was!' It was true, it *had* been Danny. Kate would never – it would never have occurred to her –

'I don't want your excuses,' said Vanessa. 'You

have a nasty dirty little mind and it's in for a big disappointment because all I went to get was his inhaler . . . He wasn't in a fit state to do what *you* were thinking. Honestly! If your mother knew some of the things that went on inside your head she'd have a fit!'

Kate really hadn't thought that Ned would make it into college that morning. When Gillian Beadle had had one of her attacks ('My Attacks') she had been off school for days on end – coddling herself, Vanessa had called it. Ned evidently didn't believe in coddling, because he was already there when Kate and Vanessa arrived. Kate was sure that he oughtn't to be, but she didn't like to say anything for fear of being thought to fuss. One or two people came up and said, 'Gosh, you look terrible!' and although Ned was polite, just as he always was, she could tell he would rather they didn't. Josh grinned and said, 'Made any obscene phone calls just lately?' which she thought was unfeeling until she remembered that Josh, of course, didn't know. Nobody did except the four of them and Mr Morrison. Mr Morrison only knew because Kate had told him. She still thought she was right, because it *wasn't* something you could hide indefinitely and Mr Morrison would only have gone on getting madder and madder, whereas now, when they met him in the corridor during the mid-morning break, he actually smiled at Ned and was quite human.

'OK?' he said. 'Well, take things easy. If it gets too much, just go and tell the office and say you're going home. You're not in the army yet. We don't want any dead heroes.'

'Get that!' said Danny, as Mr Morrison went on his way.

'Aren't we honoured?' said Vanessa.

They continued up the stairs to the refectory. They went as slowly as they could, but Ned still had to stop on the second landing to get his breath.

'You don't think you *ought* to go home, do you?' said Kate, worried. He shook his head.

'Shouldn't have come in in the first place,' said Danny. 'Dunno why he did . . . 'cos he's stubborn, that's why. Stupid, if you ask me.'

'Well, nobody did!' snapped Vanessa.

Kate and Danny looked at each other.

'Pardon me for breathing,' said Danny.

'You two go on.' Vanessa gestured, impatiently. 'We'll see you up there.'

'We'll get you a couple of coffees,' said Kate. '*Why did you let him?*' she hissed to Danny, as they bounded up the rest of the stairs.

'Let him?' said Danny. 'Are you mad?'

'He shouldn't be here.'

'Well, don't tell me,' said Danny, 'tell him!'

'All right,' said Kate. 'I will.'

She would. She would be bold and masterful. Like Vanessa. She would go up to Ned and she would say, 'Look –'

No, she wouldn't. She would say –

What would Vanessa say?

Vanessa would say: 'Look here, *I* think you ought to be at home.'

That was what Vanessa would say. Very well, then!

Kate said it. Ned just laughed. 'Don't be daft!'

'She's right,' said Danny.

'Bollocks,' said Ned.

Danny turned, deliberately, to address himself to Kate. 'Beats me,' he said, 'how he ever thinks he's going to get accepted for the bleedin' army.'

'I'll get accepted,' said Ned. 'Just so long as people don't go round shooting their mouths off.'

Kate's cheeks flared crimson for the second time that morning. Was Ned referring to her?

'Don't you go blaming Trottie!' Danny was swift to put a consoling arm round her. 'Wasn't her fault. How was she to know?'

Kate waited, fearfully, for Vanessa to say, 'I *told* her not to blab!' but Vanessa kept her eyes down and said nothing.

'Anyway,' said Danny, 'state you're in . . . what d'you think? People are blind or something? Bound to start asking questions sooner or later.'

'Yes, and surely –' Kate chipped in, eager to vindicate herself – 'surely they'd want a report from your doctor?'

'Haven't got a doctor.'

'Don't be stupid! Everybody has a flaming doctor!'

'Well, I don't go to him.'

'But he must *know*,' said Kate.

'And anyhow, you arse'ole, they'll want to examine you, won't they? Give you a medical. How d'you think you're gonna get through that?'

'I shall get through it.'

'How?'

Ned pushed a lock of hair off his forehead. 'Asthma,' he said, 'is a state of mind.'

'Looks like it!'

Ned bit his lip. Kate felt suddenly sorry for him. One shouldn't kick a person when he was down.

'Don't be rotten. You know what he means.'

'So if it's a state of mind, how come it knocks him out?'

'That's because I haven't yet learnt how to control it.'

'Yeah?'

'Don't worry,' said Ned. 'I will. After all, that's what we're here for, isn't it? Personal development . . .'

'You've got a good long way to go,' said Danny.

'I shall get there,' said Ned.

That afternoon it was Kate who had classes which went on until four-thirty and Vanessa who finished at two. Sometimes when that happened they would wait for each other and travel back together, but today Vanessa had stuck a note on Kate's locker, just as Kate, yesterday, had stuck one on hers. The note, quite simply, said SEE YOU LATER. No indications of how much later; no indication of where she had gone. Kate did her best not to feel resentful, because after all Vanessa was under no obligation to tell her where she was going. It was just that one would have thought that she would. One would have thought that it was only common politeness. Kate had, when she had gone back with Ned. She had said, in her note, GONE BACK WITH NED. (At least Vanessa couldn't have done *that*: Ned had classes until late in the afternoon.)

She half thought she might find her at home, but she hadn't arrived when Kate got back at half-past five, and still hadn't come in by half-past seven when they sat down to dinner. By eight o'clock Kate's mother had worked herself into one of her states. 'Oh, she is a naughty girl! I've told you both, always to ring. Just ring and let me know! That's all I ask.' Vanessa's father, true to form, sat behind his paper and said nothing. Vanessa, also true to form, when she did get in (at almost nine o'clock) couldn't understand what the fuss was about.

'I'm here, aren't I? It's not as if I'm *late*. I'd have told you if I were going to be late. Honestly! Anyone'd think I was a *child*.'

'You certainly behave like one,' said her father.

Vanessa pulled a rude face. She beckoned, urgently, to Kate across the room. 'Upstairs!'

'But your dinner!' wailed Kate's mother.

'Don't need it,' said Vanessa. 'I've already eaten.'

'What did you eat? When did you eat?'

'I had a pizza.'

Oh? Kate looked at her, sharply.

'Save it for tomorrow.'

'It won't keep till tomorrow! It'll just go to waste. Oh, you are a naughty girl!'

It was that sort of thoughtless behaviour which really upset Kate's mother. Kate, for once, could sympathize.

'Where have you *been*?' she said, as they went upstairs, accompanied by Jacko, to seek their usual sanctuary in Kate's bedroom. (It was cosier than Vanessa's, which tended to look a bit like an office.)

'I went back to the flat with Ned.'

'I thought he had classes?'

'He did, but he freaked out. They said he'd better go home.'

So Vanessa had taken the opportunity to go with him. Kate swallowed. I will not feel jealous, she thought. Feeling jealous was bad for you. It made you cross and unreasonable and it led to quarrels. She hadn't quarrelled with Vanessa for almost forty-eight hours now. Life was really so much pleasanter that way. And anyhow, what did she have to be jealous about? *She* was the one who had gone with him in the taxi. She was the one who'd had his head on her shoulder. She bet he hadn't put his head on Vanessa's shoulder. Brightly, she said: 'Is he all right?'

'Yes. We've been talking. He's been telling me things . . . all about when he was little, and his father being in the army and everything. I feel I understand him,' said Vanessa, 'a lot better than I did.'

'Oh?' She would *not* feel jealous. *Jealousy was unproductive.*

'This school that he went to –' Ned had told Vanessa about his *school*? 'It sounds absolutely frightful.'

'Where was it?'

'What?'

'The school! Was it somewhere famous?'

'Oh – I suppose. Yes. Quite. Anyway –'

Anyway, said Vanessa, it had been an army school, the sort of school that trained people for going into the forces, turning out *officer material* (Vanessa's lip curled as she said it). Making a *man* of you . . . 'All that sort of crap!' He'd started having asthma when he was quite little, but he'd had it specially badly after his father had been killed. For a long time they'd thought he wouldn't be able to go to his horrid school at all. But then it had seemed to clear up, everyone had thought he'd grown out of it.

Kate sat cross-legged on the bed, brow furrowed, plucking at Jacko's fur, listening to Vanessa as she talked. Ned had obviously unburdened himself – but to *Vanessa*? Ned as a rule was so guarded, he never told anyone anything about his past. How had *she* managed to get it out of him? She must have caught him in a weak moment. Kate could imagine Vanessa hammering and chiselling until she got what she wanted.

'And then, last year –'

Last year Ned had gone with his mother to the Falklands to see his father's grave and it had started everything off again, as badly as before, which just went to prove, said Vanessa, what she had maintained all along, that what he was doing wasn't right, it wasn't what he *ought* to be doing, and deep inside himself he must *know* that it wasn't what he ought to be doing, especially after that session with Morrison, 'because if he'd really been in the army he'd have *had* to carry out orders, he'd be court-martialled or something if he didn't, and anyway *why* didn't he? Because deep down he doesn't *believe* in it, that's why,' and it was about time, if you asked her, that he started to examine himself and face up to the truth and not keep pretending he was this big butch macho pig when really he wasn't at all, because nobody that was could ever have written a poem like the one Ned had written, because that poem, said Vanessa, told one *every*thing. Everything one needed to know. One only had to look at it –

Kate shifted her position slightly on the bed. She could do without a dissertation on Ned's poem. She hadn't understood a word of it.

'*Any*way –'

Vanessa, by now, was well launched. Get her astride one of her hobby horses and she would flog it half to death. Kate, massaging her right foot, which had got pins and needles, heard the words 'masculine image', '*proving* oneself', 'not letting the side down'. Jacko looked up at her and wagged, hopefully. She reminded herself that if it weren't for Vanessa, Jacko might no longer have been here.

She sighed, and forced herself to concentrate.

'. . . his mother,' said Vanessa.

'Ned's mother?' Kate perked up. This sounded more interesting. 'What about her?'

There was a pause. Kate waited, expectantly, watching Vanessa as she wandered the room, picking things up and putting them down, pressing her palm into the bristles of Kate's hairbrush, running her thumb along the teeth of Kate's comb, all with an air of concentrated abstraction. At length, picking up Kate's one and only perfume spray and spraying it into the centre of her forehead, frowning fiercely at herself in the mirror as she did so, she said: 'She's coming to London at the weekend.'

'Oh?'

'She's got some research she wants to do at the British Museum.'

'Ah.'

Pause. Vanessa put down the perfume and picked up the under-arm. Kate watched in fascination as she rubbed it over her nose. Was Vanessa *mad*?

'You know –' abruptly Vanessa swung round to face her – 'you know on Tuesdays we have a free period while Ned has economics?'

'Mm.'

'Would you come and see her with me?'

'Ned's mother?'

'Yes.'

'You mean . . . without Ned?'

'Yes.'

Kate thought about it. 'What for?'

'I want to talk to her.'

'What about?'

'Oh, Trottie, do you have to keep asking questions all the time? I didn't ask questions this morning, did I? When that brute had hold of Jacko?'

They both looked at Jacko, fast asleep with his tongue lolling out.

'I did something for *you*,' said Vanessa.

'Oh, all right,' said Kate.

'You'll come?'

'If I must.'

'And you won't say anything to Ned?'

'I suppose not.'

'Promise not!'

Kate sighed. 'I promise.'

Vanessa always got what she wanted, one way or another.

12

If experience had taught Kate anything, it was that trying to worm information out of Vanessa when she didn't want to give it was totally self-defeating. The harder you pushed, the more stubborn she became. Nevertheless, as they went in on the bus next morning, Kate made an attempt. Carelessly, with a little yawn, she said: 'What was it you wanted to talk to Ned's mother about?'

Please don't think that it matters to *me*. If she thought that it mattered to Kate, Vanessa would shut up like a clam.

She shut up like a clam anyway.

'It's not about Ned, is it?' Of course it was about Ned! Who else did she think it would be about? In sudden desperation she said, 'I hope we're not going to go poking our noses in.'

Vanessa pursed her lips. She turned, deliberately, to look out of the window. Kate's heart sank. That meant she *was* going to go poking her nose in – and Kate's nose was going to be poked in with it. This was horrible! She decided not to think about it.

Something else she had decided not to think about was her scene from *Othello*. Term ended on a Wednesday: first-year duologues were scheduled for six-thirty on the Tuesday evening. On the Friday before (which was also the Friday before Ned's mother came), they had a final rehearsal at the flat. It was disastrous. Danny fooled around, Vanessa kept bullying people, Kate forgot her lines. Ned, if such a thing were possible, was more of a cardboard cut-out than he had ever been.

'Go on,' he said to Kate. 'You can yell at me. I won't break in half. Tell me it was awful!'

It *had* been awful, but not even Vanessa could bring herself to say so. She just said bracingly that it would be all right 'on the night'.

'What makes you think so?'

'Well –' She waved a hand, confident, all embracing. 'You'll be feeling OK by then.'

'I'm feeling OK now.'

'You might be *feeling* OK, but you're still wheezing.'

'Only a bit. I might as well face it, I'm just a lousy actor – and it's poor old Trottie who's having to suffer.'

'I don't mind,' said Kate. She had resigned herself, by now, to the fact that Desdemona was not her part. On Wednesday morning, when he gave them their crits, Mr Morrison was going to tear her to pieces.

Before facing Mr Morrison, however, before even facing duologues, she had to face Ned's mother. It was not something she was looking forward to. If it hadn't been for Jacko, she would never have allowed herself to be talked into it. She spent the weekend hoping against hope that Vanessa might have forgotten, or even abandoned the idea, but Vanessa rarely forgot things and almost never abandoned any project which she herself had initiated. Kate was gloomily unsurprised, as they went home together on the Monday evening, to be informed that she had 'arranged it all'.

'I rang Ned's mother at the flat . . . we're going to meet her at ten-thirty for a coffee in that place up by the station.'

Glumly, Kate said: 'We're not supposed to leave college during study hours.'

'Well, we're going to,' said Vanessa.

Kate knew better than to argue. If Vanessa said they were going to, then they were going to. It had been just the same at the Nunnery. If Vanessa said they were going to organize an anti-apartheid demo in the front hall, then they organized an anti-apartheid demo in the front hall, in spite of Miss Woodford having expressly forbidden them to do so: if Vanessa said they were all to go on strike over lack of democratic rights, then they went on strike (and all got put on report as a result). Someone had once described Vanessa as having a forceful personality. Kate had thought, even at the time, that that was being kind: domineering was how she would have described it. And what did she want Kate there for, anyway?

She discovered what Vanessa wanted her there for as they slipped out of college at ten twenty-five next morning: she wanted her for moral support. Vanessa – self-assertive, self-assured Vanessa – was actually nervous. Kate knew she couldn't be nervous at defying authority, Vanessa had never cared tuppence for authority, and being the last person on earth to suffer from shyness she could hardly be nervous of meeting Ned's mother. That could only mean that she was nervous about what she was going to say to her. And *that* could only mean what Kate had feared all along: Vanessa was going to go poking her nose in.

Ned's mother was there before them. They knew at once it was Ned's mother, not because she looked in the least like Ned, being small and dark and rather birdlike, but because the Starlight Cafe next door to the station was not the sort of place where elegantly dressed middle-aged women were normally to be found.

'I chose it,' whispered Vanessa, 'because it was

near college.' She sounded on the defensive: a sure sign of nerves.

'Vanessa?' Mrs Carey was smiling, holding out a hand. She seemed friendly enough – *at the moment*. It would all change, thought Kate, when she discovered how interfering Vanessa could be. 'And this is – ?'

'Trottie,' said Vanessa. 'She's my sister.'

'Sort of.'

Vanessa gave a warning frown, which Kate interpreted as meaning, we can do without the double act . . . She shrugged. So let Vanessa get on with it. *She* didn't even know why they were here.

'Trottie!' said Mrs Carey. 'I've heard about Trottie from Ned.' (Oh? Kate perked up slightly.) 'Let me get you both a coffee – or would you rather have tea?'

Kate had tea and a big sticky bun. Vanessa, playing the sophisticate, had a black coffee. (She was training herself to get a taste for it.) They sat at a plastic-topped table covered in old food stains and fresh-spilt ketchup, by a flyblown window that looked out over the railway station and the Catford Road. Catford Road was a pretty dismal place to look out on at any time: in the dirt and slush of a wet December day, it was at its most unlovely. Mrs Carey glanced at it, shuddered, and looked away again.

'You'll have to excuse me,' she said. 'I'm very much a country bumpkin. I only come up to town when I absolutely have to. The Great Wen, Cobbett called it. I agree with him. Still, I suppose, when one's young –' She reached out a slender hand for her mug of tea. (Kate had to suppress an urge to giggle. She bet it wasn't every day of the week that Ned's mother partook of morning tea served in mugs the size of chamber pots.) 'Anyway, let us not waste time on idle chit-chat. What was it you wanted to see me about?'

There was a pause. Well, go on! thought Kate. Tell us! She was as much in the dark as Ned's mother.

'I wanted to ask you –'

'Yes?' Mrs Carey smiled, encouragingly.

'I wanted to ask you –'

Yes?

'About Ned.'

'Ned?' Mrs Carey sounded surprised. It occurred to Kate, somewhat belatedly, that being a well-known writer who had won prizes she had most probably thought they wanted to interview her, or get her autograph. She was probably used to people wanting to do that. This is very embarrassing, thought Kate.

Vanessa didn't appear to find it embarrassing. The possibility that Mrs Carey might have mistaken the purpose of their visit seemed not to have crossed her mind. In fact, now that she had broken the ice she was almost back to normal: back to being self-assertive and in control.

'About Ned going into the army,' she said.

'Oh.' A thin line (of displeasure?) appeared at the corner of Mrs Carey's mouth. Kate dunked her face in her mug of hot teabags. She had known Ned's mother wouldn't take kindly to interference.

'It's making him ill,' said Vanessa. She said it bluntly – almost rudely, it seemed to Kate.

'You mean by that, I take it, that he's still getting his asthma?'

'Yes. And the reason he's getting it –'

'The reason *you* think he's getting it.'

'No!' said Vanessa. 'I know! I know why he's getting it! It's because he's being torn apart – because he's being split! One half of him saying he's got to go off and be a soldier, the other half rebelling against it. *That's* what's giving it to him!'

Mrs Carey raised an eyebrow.

'Honestly,' said Vanessa.

'You sound very certain.'

'I am!' Vanessa always did sound very certain, but Mrs Carey, of course, was not to know. 'He shouldn't be doing it, it's not right for him . . . truly!'

'What makes you say so?'

'The other day –' Vanessa leaned forward, earnestly, into the tomato ketchup – 'we did this scene where we were being peace people and Ned was being a soldier.'

'Yes?'

'We were all having a go at him – yelling things, and chucking books and stuff. Then someone said she was going in – over the barrier – and Ned was told to shoot. It was an *order*.'

'And what happened?'

'He couldn't! He just couldn't *do* it – because he didn't believe in it. And it really upset him. He was really bad afterwards. Trottie actually thought he was having a heart attack, didn't you?' Vanessa swung round on Kate for confirmation. Kate mumbled incoherently into her teabags. She didn't want to be dragged into this. She hadn't wanted to come in the first place. 'Then there was that other time –' Vanessa swung back again, into the ketchup – 'that time he wrote this poem . . . all about how it would be if they dropped the bomb. It was terrifying. It was like a nightmare. It was so incredibly vivid. Of course *he* said it wasn't about the bomb, he said it was about the way he felt, inside himself –'

Did he? thought Kate.

'But if that *is* the way he feels –'

'And you think that it is.'

'I *know* that it is! He couldn't have written it if wasn't – it's not the sort of thing you can pretend about. And whether it's the bomb, or whether it's himself –'

'Doesn't really make very much difference. What you're trying to tell me is that he's a sensitive, delicate soul who has no business going into a nasty rough trade like the army.'

This is frightful, thought Kate. I should never have come.

'Honestly –' Vanessa clasped both hands to her bosom. 'I know how you feel about things – about him carrying on the family tradition and all that. Truly I do! And I think it's quite understandable, but –'

'But I don't think you do,' said Mrs Carey. She pushed her mug away. 'My dear, *I* don't need convincing that my son's not cut out to be a soldier . . . you're preaching to the converted. Ned's the one who needs convincing.'

There was a silence. Disbelieving. Vanessa stared at Ned's mother across the table.

'But he told me –'

'What did he tell you?'

'That night –' She rounded again on Kate. (Kate gulped, and almost nose-dived into her tea.) 'That night when we talked . . . do you remember? I came home and told you?' Kate nodded, anxious to appease. Vanessa swung back again to Mrs Carey. 'He told me how much it meant to you . . . how you were – oh! not exactly *relying* on him. He didn't say that.'

'I should hope not!'

'But he really thinks –' Vanessa faltered. 'He really does think –'

'That I want him to follow in his father's footsteps?' Mrs Carey shook her head. 'I begin to perceive that I have played my part too well . . . if Ned genuinely believes –' She stopped. 'I just cannot tell you how I *loathed* my husband's profession. Loathed it! I didn't always, of course. When I was young –

one doesn't always realize, when one is young. Well! Some of us don't. I'm afraid I was still very naive when I was your age. By the time I came to formulate a few positive ideas about life it was a bit late – and I suppose I felt a bit guilty. Holding the views which by then I did. It seemed . . . oh! Disloyal, I suppose. I don't think Ned's father ever guessed. I did my best to hide it from him – from everyone. I never told Ned. Not even after Anthony died, I –' She lifted a shoulder. 'I always swore that I would never try to influence Ned in any way. My own feelings were so – negative, so positively negative, it would have seemed unfair. I wanted him to feel free – to make up his own mind. Come to his own decisions. The one thing I would never have done was try to talk him out of it – I never did try to talk him out of it! But the one thing I never took into account –' The corner of her mouth turned up slightly. She had a look about her, just for a moment, of Ned. 'The one thing that never occurred to me was that silence could be so misinterpreted . . . I think perhaps in essence what you're trying to tell me is that Ned has been condemned to suffer because of my guilty conscience.'

'No!' Vanessa looked stricken. 'No, honestly, that's not what I meant!'

'It may not be what you meant, but it's nevertheless true. All those years . . . those years I played along. Never a word spoken. Never a hint dropped. And now it's come home to roost, and it's Ned who's reaping the rewards.'

Kate gazed down, troubled, into her teabags. Vanessa, plainly uncomfortable for once in her life, said: 'I'm sorry –'

'Sorry? No! Why should you be sorry? You've had the courage of your convictions – you've spoken out! Don't apologize. I salute you. The thing is . . . what's to be done?'

'It's not too late,' said Vanessa. She said it, for her, almost shyly.

'Hopefully it's not.'

'It's a question –' Vanessa stopped. She was actually blushing. 'Sorry,' she said.

'No! Go on! Tell me! You seem to be far more au fait with the workings of my son's mind than I am . . . what is it a question of?'

'I *think*,' said Vanessa, 'maybe, that what he's got to feel – if he drops the idea – is that he's dropping it for you. Rather than for himself.'

'Yes –' Mrs Carey considered the proposition. 'Yes, that makes sense . . . a little emotional blackmail, perhaps.'

'It wouldn't hurt,' said Vanessa.

'It certainly wouldn't! In fact, the more I think about it, the more I begin to feel that a little emotional blackmail is long overdue . . . on both sides! We've made each other suffer quite enough. If you knew the nightmares that I have had –' She paused. Ruefully, she said, 'If I knew the nightmares that Ned has probably had . . . I can see that I shall have to have a serious word with that young man. And the sooner the better. Let us strike while the iron is hot! He's meeting me up in town at three o'clock – I believe you have the afternoon off, is that right? You're doing things? Later on?'

Kate came to life. 'Duologues,' she said.

'Duologues! That's it. And you've to be back in college by six. I remember. Well, that gives us a couple of hours to have things out. A lot can be resolved in a couple of hours.'

'You won't tell him?' Vanessa sounded suddenly anxious. 'If he knew that we'd been talking –'

'Trust me.' Mrs Carey laid a finger to her nose. 'I shall be silent as the grave . . .'

Vanessa, on the way back to college was jubilant,

not to mention cock-a-hoop. 'There! Wasn't I right? I knew I was right! There are times when one *has* to take matters into one's own hands.'

Kate spent the afternoon with Danny, going over lines. After what had happened the other night, she had a horror of forgetting them. It was one of her worst fears, that she would dry on stage. Vanessa held that in Shakespeare it didn't matter since nobody would notice anyway. She said there had once been a famous actor-manager who, whenever his memory failed him, would cry 'Couch thee a-whilst and wait!' while he went rushing off stage to look at the book, leaving everyone else to fend for themselves.

'That's what I call presence of mind.'

Kate thought that Vanessa might call it presence of mind: Mr Morrison would probably have quite a different name for it.

'*Re-enter Emilia with Iago,*' said Danny. 'Where'd you get to after PD this morning?'

'Oh, we – er – mm . . . went for a coffee,' said Kate. 'Up the road.'

'Up the road? What d'you go up the road for?'

'Oh –' She made vague gestures in the air, trying to think of some likely-sounding explanation. If it had been left to her she would have told Danny exactly why they had gone up the road, but Vanessa had sworn her to silence and Vanessa could turn nasty if you didn't do what she had sworn you to do. Or did what she had sworn you not to do, as the case may be. 'I wanted some tights. For this evening. Why? Did someone miss us?'

'No one of any importance,' said Danny. 'Only me.'

Kate wasn't sure whether he was joking or whether he was being sarcastic. She looked at him, frowning.

'Enter Iago,' said Danny. 'Did I say that?'

She decided that all he had meant was 'only me' as opposed to someone in authority. She hoped he did. It wouldn't be like Danny to be sarcastic.

At six o'clock, as they were up in the refectory drinking last-minute cups of coffee to settle their nerves, Ned arrived back from seeing his mother.

'What's this?' he said. 'A jelly convention? I could see you all shaking from fifty yards away!'

Ned wasn't shaking – and he wasn't wheezing, either, in spite of having walked up two flights of stairs to the refectory.

'What's his game?' said Danny. 'What's he got to be all hale and hearty about?'

'Why shouldn't I be hale and hearty?' Ned pulled out a chair and sat down, next to Kate. He tweaked, playfully, at a lock of her hair. 'Good morrow, strumpet!'

'How now, my lord! What is your will?'

'Knock it off,' said Danny.

'Do you mind?' said Ned. 'We're having a rehearsal.'

'Bit late for that now,' grumbled Danny.

'Do I take it –' Vanessa, very casual, sipped at her coffee, gazing at Ned over the rim of her cup – 'that you have had a good time?'

'If you mean, am I inebriated –'

Vanessa opened wide her eyes. 'Why should I mean that?'

'– the answer is no. Not one glass of alcoholic beverage has passed my lips. If it had –' Ned turned, and made a mock snarling noise at Kate. 'Strumpet, beware!'

Kate, obliging, gave a little squeal.

'This is more than I can take,' said Danny.

'What's the matter? You want some?' Ned lunged in Danny's direction. 'Give you a kiss –'

'Gerroff!' said Danny. He jerked his thumb. 'What's got into him?'

'It's what is known as high spirits,' said Ned. 'Engendered by feelings of benevolence and good will . . . we're all invited out for a meal tonight, if you're interested. Eight o'clock, up in town.'

'What is this?' said Danny. 'Some kind of celebration?'

'Supper after the show . . . traditional, dear boy, in the best Thespian circles.'

'You what?' said Danny.

'Ac-tors,' said Ned, in Miss Truscott's voice. 'By the way, a little piece of news that will gladden the Harridan's heart . . .' He leaned across to Vanessa. 'You!' He tapped her on the back of the hand.

'Me?' said Vanessa.

'Yes. It seems you are not alone in the views that you hold.'

'Oh?'

'My mama . . . she was suddenly moved to have this great outpouring.'

'About what?'

'About the army. *Militarism*. All the sort of stuff that you usually spout.'

'Really?' Vanessa, very carefully, avoided catching Kate's eye. 'And there were you, telling me she was all for it!'

'I thought she was. As far as I was concerned . . . how was I to know? This is the first time she's ever said anything. Apparently she's been bottling it up for years. Never said a word to a soul.'

'How extraordinary,' said Vanessa. 'That poor woman! The agonies she must have suffered.'

'Well, at least she's got it off her chest now. Though why today she should suddenly decide to speak out –'

There was a pause. This time, Vanessa did catch

Kate's eye. Ned didn't notice, but Danny did. He glanced suspiciously from Kate to Vanessa, then back again to Kate.

'Will it . . . make any difference?' said Vanessa.

'Oh, absolutely! I'm now thinking of becoming a Trappist monk.'

The hands of the clock had moved to 6.16: it was time to go down to the Green Room.

'I suppose,' said Ned to Vanessa, as they left the refectory, 'you're going to crow?'

'Me?' said Vanessa. 'Why should I do that?'

'Try and claim some of the credit!'

Vanessa shook her head. 'Nothing to do with me,' she said.

Danny turned, and looked hard at Kate.

'White woman,' he hissed, 'she speak with forked tongue . . .'

Nothing would ever make Kate into the ideal Desdemona: nothing, probably, could ever transform Ned into Othello. For all that, it was not a disaster. Ned was more outgoing than Kate had yet known him: Kate, responding, was more vulnerable. She felt a glow, within herself, of achievement.

'Didn't do so badly, did we?' Ned winked at her as they left the Green Room together. 'I don't think he'll actually flog us. We mightn't get a gold star –'

'Lavatory paper,' said Kate. It was the lowest award you could get: gold star, silver star, sheet of lavatory paper.

'The fluffy kind?'

'Oh! Definitely . . . I think we deserve the fluffy kind.'

Ned grinned, and squeezed her hand. 'See you outside in ten minutes.'

Kate danced down to the cloakroom, feet on springs. Ned had winked at her, Ned had grinned at her. Ned had made snarling noises at her. Ned had squeezed her hand . . .

'You ready?' said Vanessa.

'Yes.' Kate grabbed her coat, glanced, in passing, at the mirror – stopped, and glanced again. What was that she saw? That horrid red protuberance in the middle of her chin?

A *spot????????????????*

Oh! This was too much! Why did *she* have to have spots and Vanessa not? Life was so unfair!

'Look, I'll see you outside,' said Vanessa.

'Yes. OK.'

Kate was already distracted, picking at her spot. She picked at it until it bled, until her chin felt like a piece of raw meat and she had to go and splash it in cold water. Even then it glowed an angry crimson in the fluorescent light. She could only hope that Ned's mother took them somewhere dark and fuggy where it wouldn't show. And if she could manage to sit *next* to Ned, rather than opposite –

At the top of the cloakroom stairs she found Danny, by himself.

'Where are the others?' said Kate.

'Gone. Said they'd see us at the bus stop.'

'Oh. Well – come on, then! Let's go!'

At first Kate didn't think that it was Ned and Vanessa standing at the bus stop, because she could only make out one figure. Then, as they drew nearer, she realized that the one figure was two. It was two figures locked into one. It was Ned and Vanessa, kissing . . .

They didn't even look up as Kate and Danny approached.

'Nice night,' said Danny, 'in't it?'

Kate swallowed. 'Yes,' she said. 'Lovely.'

'Bit on the cold side, p'raps.'

'Bit,' said Kate.

Danny held out a hand. 'Fancy a cuddle?'

It must have been a good five minutes before Ned and Vanessa stopped what they were doing and became aware of the world around them. Vanessa opened her eyes.

'Oh, there you are!' she said. She sounded quite aggrieved. 'We wondered where you'd got to. We've been waiting here for *ages*.'

'Imagine that,' said Danny. 'They've been waiting here for ages.'

Kate ground her teeth. The trouble with Vanessa . . .

THE END